GOD AND SATAN

Spiritual Warfare in the Bible - Volume 1

Jonathan Carl

CONTENTS

GOD AND SATAN

Spiritual Warfare in the Bible - Volume 1

God's Answers about the Battle of the Followers of
Christ against the Unseen Spiritual Forces of Evil

Dr. Jonathan Carl

Downloadable resources and helpful study videos freely available at: **www.SpiritualWarfare.blog**

I am so thankful to God for His strength and truth in Jesus! I love and am so grateful for my amazing wife Brittney and her loving, tireless support. Together we are blessed with some amazing daughters in Sophia, Lydia, Alia, and Mia! Our church family at South Fork has been incredible in their encouragement :) *Thank you all for putting up with my many hours of studying & writing for this work!*

Ephesians 6:10–12 (ESV) "Finally, be strong in the Lord and in the strength of his might. [11] Put on the whole armor of God, that you may be able to stand against the schemes of the devil. [12] For we do not wrestle against flesh and blood, but against the rulers, against the authorities, against the cosmic powers over this present darkness, against the spiritual forces of evil in the heavenly places."

ISBN-13: 9798325674631

Cover and Chapter Images by Paul Gustave Doré.

Public Domain. Accessible online at: www.wikiart.org/en/gustave-dore

than 500 consecutive verses of the ESV Bible or more than one half of any book of the ESV Bible. Accessible online at: www.esv.org

www.SpiritualWarfare.blog

www.spiritualwarfare.blog

Ephesians 6:10–12 (ESV) "Finally, be strong in the Lord and in the strength of his might. [11] Put on the whole armor of God, that you may be able to stand against the schemes of the devil. [12] For we do not wrestle against flesh and blood, but against the rulers, against the authorities, against the cosmic powers over this present darkness, against the spiritual forces of evil in the heavenly places."

Life is hard. Life is full of struggles and suffering. We need the reminder that our primary battles are not physical, financial, emotional, or mental, but spiritual. We ultimately are in an ongoing spiritual battle.

What is "spiritual warfare"? Spiritual warfare, based on Ephesians 6:12, is "the battle of the followers of Christ against the unseen spiritual forces of evil."

This resource is designed to help you find God's answers about the battle of the followers of Christ against the unseen spiritual forces of evil.

Visit our website to find freedom and victory in your daily battles through Christ's finished work on the cross. Share our free resources with others to help them as well!

www.TrustworthyWord.com

TRUSTWORTHY WORD

Titus 1:9 "He must hold firm to the trustworthy word as taught, so that he may be able to give instruction in sound doctrine and also to rebuke those who contradict it." (ESV)

Trustworthy Word was born out of a desire to equip churches with free, downloadable handouts as a resource for biblical teaching on various topics. We wanted to see the people of God think deeply about the Word of God and realize the implications that come about as a result.

One of the great things that we have seen happen though is that members of our church (South Fork Baptist Church in Hodgenville, KY) have begun to use the site as a mobile resource when they are sharing the gospel or having bible-centered conversations. Trustworthy Word has become a digital filing cabinet where with a few taps of the finger, we can quickly locate helpful resources both for our own spiritual growth and to engage those with whom we are having Christ focused conversations.

Our hope is that you too will find Trustworthy Word as a digital discipleship and evangelism resource you can utilize in moments when you have your phone, tablet, or computer with you. You may enjoy using some of the free handouts to help guide your small group into a deeper walk with Jesus in Bible study. With just a few clicks we hope you begin to think deeply about the Word of God and see how that impacts your life.

www.Bible.video - "The Video Bible"

@TheVideoBibleChannel

Bible.Video

"Until I come, devote yourself to the public reading of Scripture, to exhortation, to teaching." - 1 Timothy 4:13

Did someone read to you growing up? Did that time impact you? Help you? Grow you? Comfort you?

We feel that reading the Bible visually and audibly to one another is important and helpful too! What a joy it is to see print Bibles reaching the ends of the earth (through amazing groups like the Gideons and The International Bible Society and especially www.NetBible.com). How incredible it is that translations are made (Wycliffe) and digitally distributed (Bible.com and BibleStudyTools.com) all over the world! In the past few decades, audio Bibles have also become numerous and more accessible through wonderful ministries like Faith Comes By Hearing.

Unfortunately, there isn't much of a presence currently of someone visually reading the Bible to another. We hope to help provide this through the "The Video Bible"!

We feel this is a needed resource for evangelism

and discipleship and we pray that it will be extremely effective! The biblical origins of both visually watching someone read and listening simultaneously is important to how we process and respond to the Word.

We hope to have the opportunity to help get complete bible translations free into the ears, eyes, minds, and souls of millions more over the years ahead via video.

The**CATHOLIC** *BLOG*

www.catholic.blog

Ephesians 2:8–9 "For by grace you have been saved through faith. And this is not your own doing; it is the gift of God, not a result of works, so that no one may boast." (ESV)

What does the Catholic Church really believe? Many people have their opinions, experiences, or second-hand information on Catholic beliefs but a true understanding of the Catholic faith is found in its *Catechism of the Catholic Church*.

The Catholic Blog simply presents portions of the Catholic Catechism with relevant Bible verses and introspective questions to consider. This free resource will help you on your journey to consider the beliefs and practices of the Roman Catholic Church and examine for yourself, through tough questions, whether The Catechism of the Catholic Church is biblically valid and trustworthy.

The Catechism of the Catholic Church is a substantial document of significant history and tradition. If you have yet to read it, I encourage you to read it in its entirety. This guide should be a helpful start and reference! As you consider the "essential and fundamental contents of Catholic doctrine" (CCC, 11), I hope you will be like the Bereans of Acts 17:11 who always put the Bible first to test what they were learning.

The Bereans are described as "noble" after hearing the teaching of the Apostle Paul for two reasons:
1) getting into the Bible with "eagerness"

2) testing the teaching of the Apostle Paul in light of Scriptures to verify his truthfulness.

Similarly, may we evaluate what we see in The Catechism of the Catholic Church in the light of the Bible to "see if these things were so."

Acts 17:11 "Now these Jews were more noble than those in Thessalonica; they received the word with all eagerness, examining the Scriptures daily to see if these things were so." (ESV)

A 3 Part Approach: Here is the approach you will find to this Bible study.

1) Interesting highlights and quotes - Due to the massive volume of writings in The Catechism of the Catholic Church, I have picked quotes from the text that I think you will find most useful and fascinating.

2) Relevant Scriptures - Likewise, I selected passages of Scripture that I thought particularly helpful in evaluating and understanding the Catholic teachings. Both The Catechism of the Catholic Church and the Bible passages should be considered in their original context and setting. There are many more possible Catholic teachings and Biblical passages to consider but I hope this is a helpful start to your studies.

3) Helpful Questions - I have chosen not to insert opinions and assertions but instead propose tough questions that help us to think critically for ourselves about what we are reading.

My end goal and hope is that we all follow God's directive to us in 2 Corinthians 13:5 to "Examine yourselves, to see whether you are in the faith. Test yourselves. Or do you not realize this about yourselves, that Jesus Christ is in you?—unless indeed you fail to meet the test!" (ESV). May we all have the joy of an eternity in the presence of Jesus!

Here are the top 10 Catholic questions answered in this book with biblical answers:
1. What is the Catechism of the Catholic Church?
2. What is Sin According to the Catholic Catechism? Do Different Sins Need Different Sacrifices?
3. Does Salvation Come through Catholic Mass? Does Giving Money to Church Help Us?
4. Is Catholic Baptism Necessary for Salvation? What about Confirmation?
5. Is Catholic Eucharist Necessary for Salvation? What about Penance?

6. Was Mary Always Saved? Did Mary Never Sin? Is Mary the Cause of Salvation? Was Mary a Virgin Her Entire Life? Did Jesus Have Any Brothers? Is It True that Mary Never Died? Did Mary Ascend to Heaven?

7. Are Images of Jesus, Mary, Saints, or Angels Helpful or Harmful? Do Relics & Rosaries have Power?

8. Should We Pray to Mary and Saints? Is it OK to Pray to Angels?

9. Will I Go to Purgatory? Do Indulgences Help Us?

10. Can Marriages Be Annulled? What about Catholic Divorce and Remarriage?

Whether you are Catholic, considering Catholicism, or just curious to understand the Catholic Church better, this Bible study will be a great help to you. Download *A Biblical Study of The Catechism of the Catholic Church* free at www.Catholic.blog

INTRODUCTION

Titus 1:9 "He must hold firm to the trustworthy word as taught, so that he may be able to give instruction in sound doctrine and also to rebuke those who contradict it." (ESV)

This book is different than many others that you might read. The vast majority of the content is simply Bible verses and references. This approach, <u>with lots of bullet points</u>, is intentional in order to help you clearly hear and see God's truths and not merely human opinion. May this work be a helpful resource for your study of God's Word. May it help you increase in your love and awe of your Savior. If you aren't yet a follower of Christ, may the Lord save you through the reading of His Word throughout it!

I have used these resources in teaching my church, small groups, pastors, seminary students, and doctoral students about the subject of spiritual warfare. The source of these writings has been from my own studies, counseling with church members, and sermons. These subjects have arisen from some of the most important conversations that I have had in pastoral ministry for over a decade. I hope and pray that this work serves as a tool for the Lord to use in helping His children through His Spirit and Word.

Ultimately, I have written this for the Lord. He has grown me so much through the years and I pray that this work is faithful to honor and glorify Him. I have also always told my wife and daughters that I wrote this for them as well. I love them so much and if they were the only ones to read this, then I would count it a success!

I do hope that this is a useful Bible study resource for

many around the world. I have made these chapters, videos, and the book (and other books too) in its entirety, freely downloadable and accessible at www.SpiritualWarfare.blog and also at www.TrustworthyWord.com . It has been a joy of mine to see so many souls find Scriptural counsel online at The Spiritual Warfare Blog and Trustworthy Word over the years and I pray that it continues to aid many more until the Lord returns!

In Christ,
Jonathan Carl

Ephesians 6:17 "take the helmet of salvation, and the sword of the Spirit, which is the word of God"

OUTLINE

Here are descriptions of the other books in the series
and Scriptural reminders of their importance. The links
below contain video lectures to help you as well!

This book is a compilation of 10 other books you can find here:
www.spiritualwarfare.blog/free-books and
www.amazon.com/author/jonathancarl

- *God and Satan: Spiritual Warfare in the Bible*
- *Angels and Demons: Spiritual Warfare in the Bible*
- *Believers & Unbelievers: Spiritual Warfare in the Bible*
- *Heaven, Hell and Salvation: Spiritual Warfare in the Bible*
- *Frequently Asked Questions about Spiritual Warfare in the Bible: God's Answers about the Battle of the Followers of Christ against the Unseen Spiritual Forces of Evil*
- *Putting on God's Armor of Light: Spiritual Warfare in the Bible*
- *Resisting Satan's Schemes: Spiritual Warfare in the Bible*
- *Prayer and Fasting: Spiritual Warfare in the Bible*
- *Biblical Health: Spiritual Warfare in the Bible*
- *Evangelism and Missions: Spiritual Warfare in the Bible*

1. God & Satan
www.spiritualwarfare.blog/god-satan

Proverbs 1:7 "The fear of the LORD is the beginning of knowledge; fools despise wisdom and instruction." (ESV)

Ephesians 6:10 "Finally, be strong in the Lord and in the strength of his might." (ESV)

The story of the Bible is not a story about spiritual warfare. The story of the Bible is the story of God. As we clearly focus on who God is (His names and characteristic) and what He has done (miracles), our enemies and struggles will seem so much smaller. Although God is the Bible's primary focus, He reveals much to us about our chief enemy in Satan. Don't miss out on what God has to tell us about our enemy's names, character, and tactics that we be best prepared to live lives that enjoy and honor our Creator.

2. Angels & Demons
www.spiritualwarfare.blog/angels-demons

Colossians 1:16 "For by him all things were created, in heaven and on earth, visible and invisible, whether thrones or dominions or rulers or authorities—all things were created through him and for him." (ESV)

2 Corinthians 11:14–15 "And no wonder, for even Satan disguises himself as an angel of light. [15] So it is no surprise if his servants, also, disguise themselves as servants of righteousness. Their end will correspond to their deeds." (ESV)

God's created angels are important in the storyline of history. In Scripture God shares many stories that explain their purposes and abilities. This section will help you to rightly understand the mostly unseen angelic beings, both faithful (angels) and fallen (demons).

3. Believers & Unbelievers
www.spiritualwarfare.blog/believers-unbelievers

1 John 3:10 "By this it is evident who are the children of God, and who are the children of the devil: whoever does not practice righteousness is not of God, nor is the one who does not love his brother." (ESV)

Matthew 12:35 "The good person out of his good treasure brings forth good, and the evil person out of his evil treasure brings forth evil." (ESV)

Humanity is divided by those who follow Jesus in faith (Christian believers) and those who follow Satan, the world, and their fleshly sin (unbelievers). It is essential to understand the identities of both groups as well as the evidences of their character and works. There is no neutral ground in this battle of the followers of Christ against the spiritual forces of evil. Here are some truths to help us be aware of who we are and rightly see the world around us with a spiritual understanding.

4. Heaven & Hell and Salvation
www.spiritualwarfare.blog/heaven-hell

Romans 10:1 "Brothers, my heart's desire and prayer to God for them is that they may be saved." (ESV)

Luke 19:10 "For the Son of Man came to seek and to save the lost." (ESV)

Matthew 7:21–23 "Not everyone who says to me, 'Lord, Lord,' will enter the kingdom of heaven, but the one who does the will of my Father who is in heaven. [22] On that day many will say to me, 'Lord, Lord, did we not prophesy in your name, and cast out demons in your name, and do many mighty works in your name?' [23] And then will I declare to them, 'I never knew you; depart from me, you workers of lawlessness.'" (ESV)

God speaks clearly to us both about eternal life (Heaven) and eternal death (Hell). He wants believers to look forward to being in His presence in Heaven and also wants unbelievers to be warned of the danger of eternal suffering in Hell. Salvation is God's offer and work through Christ and He has much to tell us in the Scriptures. Here are some truths about Heaven, Hell, and God's work of salvation.

5. Spiritual Warfare Passages in the Bible
www.spiritualwarfare.blog/bible

Ephesians 6:12–13 "For we do not wrestle against flesh and blood, but against the rulers, against the authorities, against the cosmic powers over this present darkness, against the spiritual forces of evil in the heavenly places. [13] Therefore take up the whole armor of God, that you may be able to withstand in the evil day, and having done all, to stand firm." (ESV)

God warns believers about the ongoing battle between His followers and the devil's followers. He wants us to rightly understand the underlying issues of our struggles that we may daily rely on God's strength and not our own. Here are some important truths to understand about spiritual warfare.

6. Putting on God's Armor of Light
www.spiritualwarfare.blog/armor

Romans 13:12 "The night is far gone; the day is at hand. So then let us cast off the works of darkness and put on the armor of light." (ESV)

1 Thessalonians 5:8 "But since we belong to the day, let us be sober, having put on the breastplate of faith and love, and for a helmet the hope of salvation." (ESV)

God calls us to go into battle covered in His armor of light and wielding the "sword of the Spirit, which is the Word of God." This section will help you to hear God's commands and wisdom of how to live life in a way that takes into account the reality of our spiritual battles.

7. Resisting Satan's Schemes
www.spiritualwarfare.blog/schemes

Ephesians 6:11 "Put on the whole armor of God, that you may be able to stand against the schemes of the devil." (ESV)

2 Corinthians 2:11 "so that we would not be outwitted by Satan; for we are not ignorant of his designs." (ESV)

James 4:7–8 "Submit yourselves therefore to God. Resist the devil, and he will flee from you. Draw near to God, and he will draw near to you. Cleanse your hands, you sinners, and purify your hearts, you double-minded." (ESV)

God wants us to be informed of our enemy's strategies and tactics. We have a responsibility and urgent call to resist the attacks of our enemies. In this section we will hear many of the ways God shares of how to resist Satan's temptations and deception.

8. Prayer and Fasting
www.spiritualwarfare.blog/prayer

Ephesians 6:18 "praying at all times in the Spirit, with all prayer and supplication. To that end, keep alert with all perseverance, making supplication for all the saints" (ESV)

God cares for us by growing and changing us through our time with Him in prayer and fasting. As we receive God's Bible truths, we get to respond to Him and ask Him for knowledge, understanding, wisdom, and help in our times of need.

9. Biblical Health
www.spiritualwarfare.blog/health

3 John 2–4 "Beloved, I pray that all may go well with you and that you may be in good health, as it goes well with your soul. [3] For I rejoiced greatly when the brothers came and testified to your truth, as indeed you are walking in the truth. [4] I have no greater joy than to hear that my children are walking in the truth." (ESV)

God speaks to us wholistically through the Scriptures, desiring us to be healthy spiritually but also physically, mentally, emotionally, financially, relationally, and sexually. He wants us to fulfill His purposes for us in our homes, workplaces, churches and wherever we go. This section will help you to evaluate your health, identify strengths and weakness, and walk forward in God's truths for life.

10. Evangelism and Missions

www.spiritualwarfare.blog/missions

Ephesians 6:18–20 "praying ... also for me, that words may be given to me in opening my mouth boldly to proclaim the mystery of the gospel, [20] for which I am an ambassador in chains, that I may declare it boldly, as I ought to speak." (ESV)

The Christian life is a life called to love in action. We must be on the offense in sharing the hope of the Gospel news of Jesus Christ. This section will encourage and equip you to tell others about the loving life, death, and resurrection of Jesus Christ.

11. Frequently Asked Questions (FAQs)

www.spiritualwarfare.blog/faqs

1 Peter 3:15 "but in your hearts honor Christ the Lord as holy, always being prepared to make a defense to anyone who asks you for a reason for the hope that is in you; yet do it with gentleness and respect" (ESV)

Colossians 4:5–6 "Walk in wisdom toward outsiders, making the best use of the time. [6] Let your speech always be gracious, seasoned with salt, so that you may know how you ought to answer each person." (ESV)

Ephesians 4:11–14 "And he gave the apostles, the prophets, the evangelists, the shepherds and teachers, [12] to equip the saints for the work of ministry, for building up the body of Christ, [13] until we all attain to the unity of the faith and of the knowledge of the Son of God, to mature manhood, to the measure of the stature of the fullness of Christ, [14] so that we may no longer be children, tossed to and fro by the waves and carried about by every wind of doctrine, by human cunning, by craftiness in deceitful schemes." (ESV)

There are many other questions you may have that this book has not yet answered. This section will answer a few of those questions but will also challenge you to think biblically through other questions and scenarios you have already faced or that you may face in the future.

VOLUME 1: GOD & SATAN

Free Video Lectures @ www.spiritualwarfare.blog/god-satan

Proverbs 1:7 "The fear of the LORD is the beginning of knowledge; fools despise wisdom and instruction." (ESV)

Ephesians 6:10 "Finally, be strong in the Lord and in the strength of his might." (ESV)

The story of the Bible is not a story about spiritual warfare. The story of the Bible is the story of God. As we clearly focus on who God is (His names and characteristic) and what He has done (miracles), our enemies and struggles will seem so much smaller. Although God is the Bible's primary focus, He reveals much to us about our chief enemy in Satan. Don't miss out on what God has to tell us about our enemy's names, character, and tactics that we be best prepared to live lives that enjoy and honor our Creator.

"The Temptation of Jesus" by Gustave Doré

WHAT DOES THE BIBLE SAY ABOUT THE NAMES OF GOD?

"O LORD, our Lord, how majestic is your name in all the earth! You have set your glory above the heavens." Psalm 8:1 (ESV)

Our Creator (Elohim) - One God, Revealing Himself in the Three Person of Father, Son, and Spirit - Isaiah 40:28 "Have you not known? Have you not heard? The LORD is the everlasting God, the Creator of the ends of the earth. He does not faint or grow weary; his understanding is unsearchable."
- Genesis 1:1–2 "In the beginning, God created the heavens and the earth. [2] The earth was without form and void, and darkness was over the face of the deep. And the Spirit of God was hovering over the face of the waters."
- John 1:1–3 "In the beginning was the Word, and the Word was with God, and the Word was God. He was in the beginning with God. All things were made through him, and without him was not anything made that was made."

Abba, Father - Galatians 4:6 "And because you are sons, God has sent the Spirit of his Son into our hearts, crying, 'Abba! Father!'"
- Matthew 3:16–17 "And when Jesus was baptized, immediately he went up from the water, and behold, the heavens were opened to him, and he saw the Spirit of God descending like a dove and coming to rest on him; and behold, a voice from heaven said,

"This is my beloved Son, with whom I am well pleased."
· Mark 9:7 "And a cloud overshadowed them, and a voice came out of the cloud, 'This is my beloved Son; listen to him.'"

Alpha (beginning, first) & Omega (end, last) - Revelation 22:13 "I am the Alpha and the Omega, the first and the last, the beginning and the end."

Almighty (El Shaddai) - Genesis 17:1 "I am God Almighty"

Ancient of Days (Attiyq Youm) - Daniel 7:9–10 "As I looked, thrones were placed, and the Ancient of Days took his seat; his clothing was white as snow, and the hair of his head like pure wool; his throne was fiery flames; its wheels were burning fire. A stream of fire issued and came out from before him; a thousand thousands served him, and ten thousand times ten thousand stood before him; the court sat in judgment, and the books were opened."

Deliverer - Psalm 70:5 "You are my help and my deliverer; O LORD, do not delay!"

Everlasting God (El Olam) - Isaiah 40:28 "Have you not known? Have you not heard? The LORD is the everlasting God, the Creator of the ends of the earth. He does not faint or grow weary; his understanding is unsearchable."

Fortress - Psalm 18:2 "The LORD is my rock and my fortress and my deliverer, my God, my rock, in whom I take refuge, my shield, and the horn of my salvation, my stronghold."

God Most High (El Elyon) - Genesis 14:20 "blessed be God Most High, who has delivered your enemies into your hand!"

God of Knowledge (El Deah) - 1 Samuel 2:3 "the LORD is a God of knowledge, and by him actions are weighed."

God Who Gave You Birth (El Chuwl) - Deuteronomy 32:18 "the God who gave you birth"

God Who Sees (El Roi) - Genesis 16:13 "You are a God of seeing"

Great I AM - Exodus 3:14 "God said to Moses, 'I AM WHO I AM.'"

Just One - Ezra 9:15 "O LORD, the God of Israel, you are just"

Lord of All - Psalm 97:5 "The mountains melt like wax before the LORD, before the Lord of all the earth."

Lord - Our Banner (Jehovah-Nissi) - Exodus 17:15 "Moses built an altar and called the name of it, The LORD Is My Banner"

Lord - Our Creator (Jehovah-Bore) - Genesis 1:1 "In the beginning, God created the heavens and the earth."

Lord - Our Healer (Jehovah-Rapha) - Exodus 15:26 "I am the LORD, your healer."

Lord - Our Hosts (Jehovah-Sabbaoth) - Isaiah 6:3 "And one called to another and said: 'Holy, holy, holy is the LORD of hosts; the whole earth is full of his glory!'"

Lord - Our Peace (Jehovah-Shalom) - Judges 6:24 "Then Gideon built an altar there to the LORD and called it, The LORD Is Peace."

Lord - Our Provider (Jehovah-Jireh) - Genesis 22:14 "So Abraham called the name of that place, 'The LORD will provide'; as it is said to this day, 'On the mount of the LORD it shall be provided.'"

Lord - Our Righteousness (Jehovah-Tsidkenu) - Jeremiah 23:6 "In his days Judah will be saved, and Israel will dwell securely. And this is the name by which he will be called: 'The LORD is our righteousness.'"

Lord - Our Shepherd (Jehovah-Rohi) - Psalm 23:1 "The LORD is my shepherd; I shall not want."

Lord is There (Jehovah-Shammah) - Psalm 139:7 "Where shall I go from your Spirit? Or where shall I flee from your presence?"

Majestic - Psalm 8:1 O LORD, our Lord, how majestic is your name in all the earth!"

Self-Existent One (Jehovah (Yahweh)) - Exodus 3:14 "God said to Moses, "I AM WHO I AM."

Jesus - Matthew 1:21 "She will bear a son, and you shall call his name Jesus, for he will save his people from their sins."

- **Advocate** - 1 John 2:1 "we have an advocate with the Father, Jesus Christ the righteous."
- **Anointed One (Christos)** - Matthew 16:16 "Simon Peter replied, 'You are the Christ, the Son of the living God.'"
- **Author of Life** - Acts 3:15 "you killed the Author of life, whom God raised from the dead."
- **Beloved Son** - Matthew 3:17 "a voice from heaven said, "This is my beloved Son, with whom I am well pleased."
- **Bread of Life** - John 6:35 "Jesus said to them, 'I am the bread of life; whoever comes to me shall not hunger, and whoever believes in me shall never thirst.'"
- **Bridegroom** - Matthew 9:15 "And Jesus said to them, "Can the wedding guests mourn as long as the bridegroom is with them? The days will come when the bridegroom is taken away from them, and then they will fast."
- **Bright Morning Star** - Revelation 22:16 "I, Jesus, have sent my angel to testify to you about these things for the churches. I am the root and the descendant of David, the bright morning star."
- **Chief Shepherd** - 1 Peter 5:4 "And when the chief Shepherd appears, you will receive the unfading crown of glory."
- **Cornerstone** - Mark 12:10 "The stone that the builders rejected has become the cornerstone"
- **Door** - John 10:9 "I am the door. If anyone enters by me, he will be saved"
- **Faithful Witness** - Revelation 1:5 "Jesus Christ the faithful witness, the firstborn of the dead, and the ruler of kings on earth. To him who loves us and has freed us from our sins by his blood"
- **Founder (author) & Perfecter (finisher) of Our Faith**- Hebrews 12:2 "looking to Jesus, the founder and perfecter of our faith, who for the joy that was set before him endured the cross, despising the shame, and is seated at the right hand of the throne of God."

- **Founder (Captain) of our Salvation** - Hebrews 2:10 "the founder of their salvation"
- **God** - Colossians 2:9 "For in him the whole fullness of deity dwells bodily"
    - Romans 9:5 "the Christ, who is God over all"
    - John 14:9–10 "Whoever has seen me has seen the Father … I am in the Father & the Father is in me"
    - John 10:30 "I and the Father are one."
- **Good Shepherd** - John 10:11 "I am the good shepherd. The good shepherd lays down his life for the sheep."
- **Great High Priest** - Hebrews 4:14 "Since then we have a great high priest who has passed through the heavens, Jesus, the Son of God, let us hold fast our confession."
- **Head of the Church** - Ephesians 5:23 "Christ is the head of the church, his body, and is himself its Savior."
- **Image of the Invisible God** - Colossians 1:15 "He is the image of the invisible God"
    - 2 Corinthians 4:4 "Christ, who is the image of God. (ESV)
- **Immanuel** - Matthew 1:23 "Behold, the virgin shall conceive and bear a son, and they shall call his name Immanuel" (which means, God with us)."
- **Judge** - Acts 10:42 "he is the one appointed by God to be judge of the living and the dead."
- **King of Kings, Lord of Lords** - Revelation 17:14 "the Lamb will conquer them, for he is Lord of lords and King of kings, and those with him are called and chosen and faithful."
- **Lamb of God** - John 1:29 "Behold, the Lamb of God, who takes away the sin of the world!"
- **Light of the World** - John 8:12 "I am the light of the world. Whoever follows me will not walk in darkness, but will have the light of life."
- **Lion of Judah** - Revelation 5:5 "Weep no more; behold, the Lion of the tribe of Judah, the Root of David, has conquered, so that he can open the scroll and its seven seals."
- **Living Water** - John 4:14 "whoever drinks of the water that

I will give him will never be thirsty again. The water that I will give him will become in him a spring of water welling up to eternal life."

- **Lord of Glory** - James 2:1 "hold the faith in our Lord Jesus Christ, the Lord of glory"
- **Man of Sorrows** - Isaiah 53:3 "He was despised and rejected by men, a man of sorrows and acquainted with grief; and as one from whom men hide their faces he was despised, and we esteemed him not."
- **Mediator** - 1 Timothy 2:5 "there is one mediator between God and men, the man Christ Jesus"
- **Messiah** - John 1:41 "'We have found the Messiah' (which means Christ)."
- **Name Above All Names** - Philippians 2:9 "Therefore God has highly exalted him and bestowed on him the name that is above every name"
- **Only Son** - John 3:16 "For God so loved the world, that he gave his only Son, that whoever believes in him should not perish but have eternal life."
- **The Power of God, The Wisdom of God** - 1 Corinthians 1:23–24 "we preach Christ crucified… the power of God and the wisdom of God."
- **Prophet** - John 6:14 "When the people saw the sign that he had done, they said, 'This is indeed the Prophet who is to come into the world!'"
- **Redeemer** - Job 19:25 "For I know that my Redeemer lives, and at the last he will stand upon the earth."
- **Resurrection** - John 11:25–26 "Jesus said to her, 'I am the resurrection and the life. Whoever believes in me, though he die, yet shall he live, and everyone who lives and believes in me shall never die. Do you believe this?'"
- **Rock** - 1 Corinthians 10:4 "they drank from the spiritual Rock that followed them, and the Rock was Christ."
- **Savior** - 1 John 4:14 "we have seen and testify that the Father has sent his Son to be the Savior of the world."
- **Son of God** - 1 John 5:13 "I write these things to you who

believe in the name of the Son of God, that you may know that you have eternal life."

- **Son of Man** - Matthew 20:28 "the Son of Man came not to be served but to serve, and to give his life as a ransom for many."
- **Teacher/Master** - John 13:13 "You call me Teacher and Lord, and you are right, for so I am."
- **True Light** - John 1:9 "The true light, which gives light to everyone, was coming into the world."
- **True Vine** - John 15:1 "I am the true vine, and my Father is the vinedresser."
- **Word of God** - John 1:14 "the Word became flesh and dwelt among us, and we have seen his glory, glory as of the only Son from the Father, full of grace and truth."
- **The Way, The Truth, The Life** - John 14:6 "Jesus said to him, 'I am the way, and the truth, and the life. No one comes to the Father except through me.'"
- **Wonderful Counselor, Mighty God, Everlasting Father, Prince of Peace** - Isaiah 9:6 "For to us a child is born, to us a son is given; and the government shall be upon his shoulder, and his name shall be called Wonderful Counselor, Mighty God, Everlasting Father, Prince of Peace."
- **Yahweh (Jehovah) - I AM** - John 8:58 "Jesus said to them, 'Truly, truly, I say to you, before Abraham was, I am.'"

Spirit - John 4:24 "God is spirit, and those who worship him must worship in spirit and truth."

- **Breath of the Almighty** - Job 33:4 "The Spirit of God has made me, and the breath of the Almighty gives me life."
- **Helper** - John 14:16 "And I will ask the Father, and he will give you another Helper, to be with you forever"
- **Spirit of Counsel & Might** - Isaiah 11:2 "And the Spirit of the LORD shall rest upon him ... the Spirit of counsel and might"
- **Spirit of Adoption** - Romans 8:15 - "For you did not receive the spirit of slavery to fall back into fear, but you have received the Spirit of adoption as sons, by whom we cry, 'Abba! Father!'"
- **Spirit of Judgment & Burning** - Isaiah 4:4 "when the Lord shall have washed away the filth of the daughters of Zion and cleansed the bloodstains of Jerusalem from its midst by a spirit of judgment and by a spirit of burning."
- **Spirit of Christ** - 1 Peter 1:10–11 "Concerning this salvation, the prophets who prophesied about the grace that was to be yours searched and inquired carefully, inquiring what person or time the Spirit of Christ in them was indicating when he predicted the sufferings of Christ and the subsequent glories."
  - Romans 8:9 "You, however, are not in the flesh but in the Spirit, if in fact the Spirit of God dwells in you. Anyone who does not have the Spirit of Christ does not belong to him."
- **Spirit of Glory** - 1 Peter 4:14 "If you are insulted for the name of Christ, you are blessed, because the Spirit of glory and of God rests upon you."
- **Spirit of God** - Genesis 1:2 "The earth was without form and void, and darkness was over the face of the deep. And the Spirit of God was hovering over the face of the waters."
- **Spirit of Grace** - Zechariah 12:10 "And I will pour out on the house of David and the inhabitants of Jerusalem a spirit of grace and pleas for mercy, so that, when they look on me, on him whom they have pierced, they shall mourn for him, as one mourns for an only child, and weep bitterly over him, as one weeps over a firstborn."

- **Spirit of Knowledge & the Fear of the Lord** - Isaiah 11:2 "And the Spirit of the LORD shall rest upon him ... the Spirit of knowledge and the fear of the LORD."
- **Spirit of Truth** - John 14:17 "the Spirit of truth, whom the world cannot receive, because it neither sees him nor knows him. You know him, for he dwells with you and will be in you."
- **Spirit of Wisdom & Understanding** - Isaiah 11:2 "And the Spirit of the LORD shall rest upon him ... the Spirit of wisdom and understanding"
- **Spirit of Life** - Romans 8:2 "the law of the Spirit of life has set you free in Christ Jesus from the law of sin and death."
- **Spirit of the Living God** - 2 Corinthians 3:3 "you show that you are a letter from Christ delivered by us, written not with ink but with the Spirit of the living God, not on tablets of stone but on tablets of human hearts."
- **Spirit of Prophecy** - Revelation 19:10 "For the testimony of Jesus is the spirit of prophecy."
- **Spirit of Revelation** - Ephesians 1:17 "that the God of our Lord Jesus Christ, the Father of glory, may give you the Spirit of wisdom and of revelation in the knowledge of him"
- **Spirit of the Father** - Matthew 10:20 "For it is not you who speak, but the Spirit of your Father speaking through you."
- **Spirit of Son** - Galatians 4:6 "And because you are sons, God has sent the Spirit of his Son into our hearts, crying, 'Abba! Father!'"

Helpful Resources For Studying The Names Of God:

- *God Is* by Ken Hemphill
- **GotQuestions.org**
    What are the names of God and what do they mean? www.gotquestions.org/names-of-God.html
    What are the names of Jesus? www.gotquestions.org/names-Jesus-Christ.html

What are the names of the Holy Spirit?
www.gotquestions.org/names-Holy-Spirit.html

What does the Bible teach about the Trinity?
www.gotquestions.org/Trinity-Bible.html

- **"Names of God" by Adrian Rogers** (www.lwf.org/names-of-god)
- **Rose Publishing** - www.hendricksonrose.com

Attributes of God, I Am, Names of God, Names of Jesus, Names of Holy Spirit

WHAT DOES THE BIBLE SAY ABOUT THE MIRACLES OF GOD?

The Most Important
Miracles in the Bible

What does the Bible say about the wonderful works of God?
Psalm 9:1 "I will give thanks to the LORD with my whole heart;
I will recount all of your wonderful deeds." (ESV)

1. Creation of the Universe from Nothing - Day and Night - Sky - Sea, Land, Plants, and Trees - Sun, Moon, and Stars - Birds and Fish - Animals and Humans (Genesis 1-2)
2. Enoch Taken Up to God without Dying (Genesis 5:24, Hebrews 11:5)
3. The Global Flood and Noah's Salvation (Genesis 7-8)
4. Creation of Languages at Babel (Gen 11:1-9)
5. Abraham's Covenant Sacrifice Passed through by a Smoking Fire Pot and a Flaming Torch (Genesis 15:17)
6. God Appears (theophany) or Sends Angels
•   (Genesis 16:7–14 to Hagar, Genesis 22:11–15 to Abraham, Genesis 31:11 to Jacob, Exodus 3:2–4, Exodus 19-34 to Moses, Exodus 23:20–21, 33:2, Numbers 20:16 an Angel before the Israelites, Numbers 22:22–38 to Balaam, Judges 2:1–3 to all the people of Israel, Judges 6:11–23 to Gideon, Judges 13:3–22 to

Manoah and his wife, 1 Chronicles 21:15 to destroy Jerusalem, 1 Samuel 3 to Samuel, 2 Samuel 24:16-17 to David, 1 Kings 19, 2 Kings 1 to Elijah, Zechariah 1-6 angelic visions to Zechariah, Zechariah 3:4 The angel of the Lord takes away the sin of the high priest Joshua, Luke 1:11-20)

7. Destruction of Sodom & Gomorrah with Fire and Stone (Genesis 19:4)
8. Lot's Wife Turned into a Pillar of Salt (Genesis 19:26)
9. Birth of Isaac to Sarah (90 years old) and Abraham (100 years old) (Genesis 21:1)
10. Burning Bush Unconsumed (Exodus 3:3)
11. Aaron's Staff Turns into a Serpent (Exodus 7:10-12)
12. Plagues of Egypt (Water to blood, frogs, gnats, flies, livestock plague, boils, thunder & hail, locusts, darkness, & death of the first-born) (Exodus 7:20-12:3)
13. The Lord & the Angel of God Lead Israel by Pillar of Cloud and Fire (Ex13:21-22, 14:19-20)
14. God's Presence on Mt. Sinai (Genesis 19:16-20, 20:18, 24:9-11)
15. Moses Face Shining (Exodus 34:29-35)
16. God's Presence in the Tabernacle Seen by Cloud and Fire (Exodus 33:9-10; 40:34-38)
17. Parting of the Red Sea (Exodus 14:21)
18. Waters of Marah Cleansed (Exodus 15:23-25)
19. Bread and Quail from Heaven (Exodus 16:14-35)
20. Water from Rock (Exodus 17:5)
21. 40 Years in the Desert - No Worn-Out Clothes, No Swollen Feet (Deuteronomy 8:4)
22. Fire Consumes Nadab and Abihu (Leviticus 10:1-2)
23. Fire Sent Against Complaining (Numbers 11:1-3)
24. Earth Opens Up Beneath the people of Korah (Numbers 16:32)
25. Fire Consumes 250 (Numbers 16:35-45)
26. Plague Kills 14,700 Complainers Against Moses and Aaron (Numbers 16:46-50)
27. Aaron's Rod Buds with Almonds (Numbers 17:8)

28. Water from Rock (Numbers 20:7-11)
29. Impatience and Complaining Against God Is Punished by Serpents, Healed Found by Looking at a Bronze Serpent Raised on a Pole (Numbers 21:4-9, 2 Kings 18:4, John 3:14–15)
30. Balaam's Donkey Speaks (Numbers 22:21-35)
31. Parting of the Jordan River (Joshua 3:14)
32. Jericho's Walls Fall Down (Joshua 6:6-20)
33. The Lord Kills by Hailstones (Joshua 10:11)
34. The Earth's Rotation Stops - Sun and Moon Stand Still (Joshua 10:12-14)
35. Gideon's Fleece Wet and Dry (Judges 6:37-40)
36. Samson's Supernatural Strength (Judges 14-16)
37. Water Emerges from the Ground for Samson (Judges 15:19)
38. Dagon Idol Falls & Breaks Before the Ark of the Covenant (1 Samuel 5:1-5)
39. Tumors Come Upon the Philistines (1 Samuel 5:6-12)
40. 70 Killed for Looking at the Ark (1 Samuel 6:19)
41. Thunder Sent to Destroy the Philistines in Battle (1 Samuel 7:10)
42. Lord Sends Thunder and Rain at Samuel's Request (1 Samuel 12:18)
43. David Defeats Goliath (1 Samuel 17)
44. Lord Sends Sound to Show David His Victory (2 Samuel 5:23-25)
45. Uzzah Killed for Touching the Ark (2 Samuel 6:6-7)
46. King Jeroboam's Hand Is Withered and Healed (1 Kings 13:4-6)
47. Ravens Feed Elijah (1 Kings 17:1-7)
48. Widow's Flour and Oil Multiplies with Elijah (1 Kings 17:14-16)
49. Elijah Raises the Widow's Son from the Dead (1 Kings 17:17-24)
50. Elijah's Words Brings Drought and then Rain (1 Kings 17-18)

51. Fire on Mt. Carmel, Prophets of Ba'al Defeated (1 Kings 18:20-40)
52. Elijah's Running Faster than King Ahab's Chariot (1 King 18:46)
53. Elijah Given a Hot Meal and Water from an Angel (1 Kings 19:6)
54. Fire Consumes 102 Soldiers at Elijah's Command (2 Kings 1:10-16)
55. Elijah and Elisha Part the Jordan River with a Cloak (2 Kings 2:7-8, 14)
56. Elijah Carried to Heaven (2 Kings 2:11)
57. Elisha Purifies Jericho's Water Supply (2 Kings 2:21-22)
58. Elisha Curses 42 Young Men for Mocking Elisha as a Prophet of God, they are Mauled by Bears (2 Kings 2:24)
59. Elisha Prophecies the Provision of Water for the Israelite Army in the Desert (2 Kings 3:16-22)
60. Elisha Provides Multiplication of Oil for a Widow's Debt (2 Kings 4:1-7)
61. Elisha Prophecies for a Birth, Raises Shunammite's Son from the Dead (2 Kings 4:14-37)
62. Elisha Heals a Deadly Pot of Stew (2 Kings 4:38-41)
63. Elisha Multiplies 20 Loaves to Feed 100, with Leftovers (2 Kings 4:42-44)
64. Elisha Heals Naaman of Leprosy in the Jordan River, Gehazi's Greed is Punished with Leprosy (2 Kings 5)
65. Elisha Makes an Ax-head Float (2 Kings 6:5-7)
66. Elisha Knows the King Syria's Plans (2 Kings 6:12)
67. Elisha Asks for His Servant to See the Lord's Army of Horses and Chariots (2 Kings 6:17)
68. Elisha Prays for the Syrian Army to Be Blinded and then have their Sight Restored (2 Kings 6:18-20)
69. Elisha's Bones Resurrect a Dead Man (2 Kings 13:21)
70. Lions Sent by the Lord to Kill the Assyrians (2 Kings 17:25)
71. God Destroys 185,000 Assyrians (2 Chronicles 32:21, 2 Kings 19:35)

72. Isaiah and Hezekiah Ask God to Move the Sun Dial Shadow Backwards 10 Degrees (2 Kings 20:9-11)
73. King Uzziah Pridefully Enters the Temple and becomes a Leper (2 Chronicles 26:16-21)
74. Daniel, Shadrach, Meshach, & Abednego Given Supernatural Health & Wisdom for Faithful Fasting (Daniel 1:8-21)
75. Delivers Shadrach, Meshach, & Abednego in the Fiery Furnace (Daniel 3:16-30)
76. King Nebuchadnezzar Loses Mind from Pride and Regains Mind when Humbled (Daniel 4:28-37)
77. Handwriting on the Wall in front of King Belshazzar of Babylon (Daniel 5:5)
78. Delivers Daniel in the Lion's Den (Daniel 6:22)
79. Jonah in the Belly of a Whale (Jonah 2:1-10)
80. Gabriel and other Angels Appear to Mary, Joseph, Zechariah, and the Shepherds (Luke 1:11-20, Luke 1:26-38, Luke 2:8-15, Matthew 1:20-25, Matthew 2:19)
81. Virgin Birth of Jesus (Matthew 1:18-25, Luke 1:26-38)
82. Star of Bethlehem Leads Wise Men to Jesus (Matthew 2:1-12)
83. 300+ Prophecies Fulfilled about Jesus - www.trustworthyword.com/evidence-for-jesus
84. Angels Minister to Jesus After Satan's Temptations (Matthew 4:11)
85. God the Father's Voice Heard and God the Spirit's Presence Seen at Jesus' Baptism (Matthew 3:13-17)
86. Jesus Turns Water into Wine (John 2:1-11)
87. Jesus Heals an Official's Son (John 4:43-54)
88. Jesus Escapes from a Murderous Mob in His Hometown of Nazareth (Luke 4:30)
89. Jesus Casts Out a Demon at Capernaum (Mark 1:21-27, Luke 4:31-36)
90. Jesus Heals Peter's Sick Mother-In-Law (Matthew 8:14-15, Mark 1:29-31, Luke 4:38-39)
91. Jesus Heals Many who are Sick and Demonically

Oppressed (Matthew 8:16-17, Mark 1:32-34, Luke 4:40-41)

92. Jesus Gives Peter, James, and John a Miraculous Catch of Fish (Luke 5:1-11)

93. Jesus Cleanses a Man with Leprosy (Matthew 8:1-4, Mark 1:40-45, Luke 5:12-14)

94. Jesus Heals a Centurion's Paralyzed Servant (Matthew 8:5-13, Luke 7:1-10)

95. Jesus Heals a Paralytic Let Down from the Roof by Friends (Matthew 9:1-8, Mark 2:1-12, Luke 5:17-26)

96. Jesus Heals a Man's Withered Hand on the Sabbath (Matthew 12:9-14, Mark 3:1-6, Luke 6:6-11)

97. Jesus Raises a Widow's Son from the Dead (Luke 7:11-17)

98. Jesus Calms a Storm on the Sea of Galilee (Matthew 8:23-27, Mark 4:35-41, Luke 8:22-25)

99. Jesus Casts Out Demons out of a Man and into a Herd of Pigs (Matthew 8:28-33, Mark 5:1-20, Luke 8:26-39)

100. Jesus Heals a Woman with an Issue of Blood (Matthew 9:20-22, Mark 5:25-34, Luke 8:42-48)

101. Jesus Raises Jarius' Daughter Back to Life (Matthew 9:18, 23-26, Mark 5:21-24, 35-43, Luke 8:40-42, 49-56)

102. Jesus Heals Two Blind Men (Matthew 9:27-31)

103. Jesus Heals a Mute Man (Matthew 9:32-34)

104. Jesus Heals a Man Unable to Walk (John 5:1-15)

105. Jesus Feeds 5,000 Men Plus Many Women and Children (Matthew 14:13-21, Mark 6:30-44, Luke 9:10-17, John 6:1-15)

106. Jesus Walks on Water (Matthew 14:22-33, Mark 6:45-52, John 6:16-21)

107. Jesus Heals Everyone Who Touches His Clothing (Matthew 15:21-28, Mark 7:24-30)

108. Jesus Casts a Demon from a Foreign Woman's Daughter (Matthew 15:21-28, Mark 7:24-40)

109. Jesus Heals a Deaf Man with a Speech Impediment (Mark 7:31-37)

110. Jesus Feeds 4,000 Plus Women and Children (Matthew 15:32-39, Mark 8:1-13)
111. Jesus Heals a Blind Man with Spit at Bethsaida (Mark 8:22-26)
112. Jesus Heals a Blind Man with Mud and Washing at Siloam (John 9:1-12)
113. God the Father's Voice Heard at Jesus' Transfiguration (Matthew 17:1–8, Mark 9:2–8, Luke 9:28–36)
114. Jesus Casts a Demon Out of a Mute Boy Suffering from Harmful Seizures (Matthew 17:14-20, Mark 9:14-29, Luke 9:37-43)
115. 72 Disciples Empowered Over the Demonic (Luke 10:17-20)
116. Jesus Pulls the Temple Tax (a Coin Shekel) from a Fish's Mouth (Matthew 17:24-27)
117. Jesus Casts a Demon Out of a Blind and Mute Man (Matthew 12:22-23, Luke 11:14-23)
118. Jesus Heals a Crippled Woman (Luke 13:10-17)
119. Jesus Heals a Man with Excessive Swelling (Dropsy/ Edema) (Luke 14:1-6)
120. Jesus Heals Ten People with Leprosy (Luke 17:11-19)
121. Jesus Raises Lazarus from the Dead (John 11:1-45)
122. God the Father's Voice Speaks Over His Son (John 12:28)
123. Jesus Heals a Blind Beggar (Bartimaeus) (Matthew 20:29-34, Luke 10:46-52, Luke 18:35-43)
124. Jesus Curses & Withers an Unproductive Fig Tree (Matthew 21:18-22, Mark 11:12-14)
125. Angels Strengthen Jesus in the Garden of Gethsemane (Luke 22:43)
126. Jesus Heals a Servant's (Malchus') Severed Ear in the Garden of Gethsemane (Luke 22:50-51)
127. Supernatural Darkness Covers the Land for the Three Hours Immediately Prior to Jesus' Death (Matthew 27:45)
128. The Curtain of the Temple Tears in Two at the Moment

of Jesus' Death (Matthew 27:51)

129. An Earthquake Occurs at the Moment of Jesus' Death (Matthew 27:51)

130. Many Dead Believers Are Resurrected at the Moment of Jesus' Death (Matthew 27:52-53)

131. An Earthquake Occurs at the Moment of Jesus' Resurrection (Matthew 28:2)

132. Jesus Is Resurrected (Matthew 28, Mark 16, Luke 24, John 20, 1 Corinthians 15)

133. Angels Appear at Jesus' Tomb Upon His Resurrection (Matthew 28:2-7, John 20:12-13)

134. Jesus Enters a Locked Room in Jerusalem (John 20:19)

135. Jesus Breathes Out the Holy Spirit Upon His Disciples (John 20:22)

136. Jesus Vanishes from the Presence of Two Disciples (Luke 24:31)

137. Jesus Gives Peter and the Disciples a Second Miraculous Catch of Fish (John 21:4-11)

138. Jesus Ascends Into Heaven (Acts 1:9-11)

139. Angels at Jesus' Ascension (Acts 1:10-11)

140. Sound of Rushing Wind, Tongues of Fire (Acts 2:1-2)

141. Ability to Speak and Be Understood by Many Languages (Tongues) (Acts 2:4-13)

142. Peter Heals a Man Unable to Walk (Acts 3:1-10)

143. Peter and John Speak with Boldness and the Place was Shaken (Acts 4:28-31)

144. Ananias and Sapphire Die for Lying to the Holy Spirit (Acts 5:1-11)

145. Peter Heals Many of Diseases and Demons, Even through His Shadow (Acts 5:12-16)

146. Angelic Opening of the Prison Doors to Free Apostles (Acts 5:19) opening the prison doors to free the Apostles,

147. Stephen's Wonders and Signs (Acts 6:8)

148. Stephen Sees the Glory of God and Jesus Standing by His Father (Acts 7:55-56)

149. Philip Casts Out Demons and Heals the Paralyzed and Lame (Acts 8:6-7)
150. Angel Tells Philip to Go South (Acts 8:26)
151. Spirit Tells Philip to Go to the Ethiopian Eunuch's Chariot (Acts 8:29)
152. Spirit Transports Philip from the Desert to Azotus (Acts 8:39)
153. God Appears to Paul and Ananias (Acts 9:1-19)
154. Paralytic (Aeneas) Healed by Peter (Acts 9:32-35)
155. Tabitha (Dorcas) Raised from the Dead (Acts 9:36-43)
156. Angel of God Appears to Centurion Cornelius and the Lord Speaks to Peter (Acts 10:1-16)
157. Gentiles Receive the Holy Spirit and Speak in Languages (Acts 10:44-48)
158. Agabus Prophecies about a Future Famine & Paul's Imprisonment (Acts 11:28, Acts 21:10-12)
159. An Angel of the Lord delivers Peter from prison (Acts 12:7-10)
160. An Angel of the Lord Strikes Down & Kills King Herod for Not Glorifying God (Acts 12:22-23)
161. Elymas the Magician is Blinded (Acts 13:8-12)
162. Paul Heals a Lame Man (Acts 14:8-10)
163. Paul's Vision to Go to Macedonia (Acts 16:9)
164. Paul Casts Out a Demon from a Fortune-Telling Slave Girl (Acts 16:16-18)
165. Paul and Silas Prison Doors and Shackles Opened by an Earthquake (Acts 16:25-34)
166. The Holy Spirit Falls on New Believers in Ephesus, Evidenced by Languages (tongues) and Prophesy (Acts 19:5-6)
167. Paul Heals and Casts Out Demons, even through handkerchiefs (Acts 19:11-12)
168. Eutychus Raised to Life (Acts 20:7-12)
169. Angel Speaks to Paul with Warning Prior to a Shipwreck (Acts 27:23-24)
170. Paul Bitten by a Viper but Unharmed (Acts 28:1-6)

171. Paul Heals Many on Malta (Acts 28:7-10)
172. Continuation of Spiritual Gifts in the Church - Spirit of Utterance of Wisdom and Knowledge, Faith, Gifts of Healing, Working of Miracles, Prophecy, Ability to Distinguish Spirits, Ability to Speak and Interpret Language (1 Corinthians 12:1-11)
173. The Power of Signs, Wonders, Mighty Works, Miracles, and Gifts Referenced (Romans 12:6-8, Romans 15:17-19, 2 Corinthians 12:1-29, Hebrews 2:4, Galatians 3:5, 1 Corinthians 14)
174. John's Vision on Patmos (the book of Revelation)
175. Many More Miracles of Jesus Not Recorded (John 20:30, Acts 10:38-39)
176. Many More Miracles Yet to Come (Matthew 13:29-49, Matthew 16:27, 24:31, 25:31, Revelation)

WHAT DOES THE BIBLE SAY ABOUT THE CHARACTER OF GOD?

What Does the Bible Say God is Like?

The Character & Attributes of God

Romans 1:20 "For his invisible attributes, namely, his eternal power and divine nature, have been clearly perceived, ever since the creation of the world, in the things that have been made. So they are without excuse." (ESV)

1. **A Unity** - "Hear, O Israel: The LORD our God, the LORD is one. (Deut 6:4)
2. **Beautiful** - "to gaze upon the beauty of the Lord" (Psalm 27:4)
3. **Blessed** – "God saw everything that he had made, and behold, it was very good." (Genesis 1:31)
4. **Creator, Source of Life** - "In the beginning, God created the heavens and the earth." (Gen 1:1); "All things were made through him, and without him was not any thing made that was made." (John 1:3)
5. **Divine** - "But the LORD is the true God; he is the living God and the everlasting King. At his wrath the earth quakes, and the nations cannot endure his indignation." (Jeremiah 10:10)
6. **Eternal, Preexistent** – "Before the mountains were brought

forth, or ever you had formed the earth and the world, from everlasting to everlasting you are God." (Psalm 90:2)

7. **Faithful** - "If we confess our sins, he is faithful and just to forgive us our sins and to cleanse us from all unrighteousness." (1 John 1:9)

8. **Freedom** – "Our God is in the heavens; he does all that he pleases." (Psalm 115:3)

9. **Good** – "No one is good except God alone" (Luke 18:19)

10. **Gracious and Merciful** - "Nevertheless, in your great mercies you did not make an end of them or forsake them, for you are a gracious and merciful God." (Nehemiah 9:31)

11. **Holy** – "Holy, holy, holy, is the Lord of hosts." (Isaiah 6:3)

12. **Independent** - "The God who made the world and everything in it, being Lord of heaven and earth, does not live in temples made by man, nor is he served by human hands, as though he needed anything, since he himself gives to all mankind life and breath and everything." (Acts 17:24-25)

13. **Innocent** - "Let no one say when he is tempted, 'I am being tempted by God,' for God cannot be tempted with evil, and he himself tempts no one. But each person is tempted when he is lured and enticed by his own desire." (James 1:13-14); "'Naked I came from my mother's womb, and naked shall I return. The LORD gave, and the LORD has taken away; blessed be the name of the LORD.' [22] In all this Job did not sin or charge God with wrong." (Job 1:21-22)

14. **Invisible** – "No one has ever [fully] seen God" (John 1:18)

15. **Jealous** – "I the Lord your God am a jealous God" (Exodus 20:5)

16. **Just Judge** - "And just as it is appointed for man to die once, and after that comes judgment" (Hebrews 9:27)

17. **Knowable** - "but let him who boasts boast in this, that he understands and knows me" (Jeremiah 9:24)

18. **Love** – "God is love" (1 John 4:8)

19. **Omnipotent** – "with God all things are possible" (Matthew 19:26)

20. **Omnipresent** – "Where shall I go from your Spirit? Or where shall I flee from your presence?" (Psalm 139:7)

21. **Omniscient** – "He knows everything" (1 John 3:20)

22. **Perfect** – "your heavenly Father is perfect." (Matthew 5:48)

23. **Righteous and Just** – "All his ways are justice. A God of faithfulness and without iniquity, just and upright is he." (Deuteronomy 32:4)

24. **Sovereign** - "Oh, the depth of the riches and wisdom and knowledge of God! How unsearchable are his judgments and how inscrutable his ways! [34] 'For who has known the mind of the Lord, or who has been his counselor?' [35] 'Or who has given a gift to him that he might be repaid?'[36] For from him and through him and to him are all things. To him be glory forever. Amen." (Romans 11:33-36)

25. **Spirit** – "God is spirit" (John 4:24)

26. **Strength** - "that according to the riches of his glory he may grant you to be strengthened with power through his Spirit in your inner being" (Ephesians 3:16)

27. **Truthful** – "The Lord is the true God" (Jeremiah 10:10)

28. **Unchangeable** - "For I the Lord do not change" (Malachi 3:6)

29. **Wills** – "if the Lord wills, we will live and do this or that." (James 4:15); "according to the purpose of him who works all things according to the counsel of his will" (Ephesians 1:11)

30. **Wise** – "the only wise God" (Romans 16:27)

31. **Worthy** - "And they sang a new song, saying, 'Worthy are you to take the scroll and to open its seals, for you were slain, and by your blood you ransomed people for God from every tribe and language and people and nation, [10] and you have made them a kingdom and priests to our God, and they shall reign on the earth." (Revelation 5:9–10)

32. **Wrathful Towards Sin** – "Whoever does not obey the Son shall not see life, but the wrath of God remains on

him." (John 3:36)

Helpful resources:

- "What is the character of God" - www.gotquestions.org/character-of-God.html
- Wayne Grudem's *Christian Beliefs*

The Greatest Modern-Day Identity Theft

*10 Misrepresentations of the Character of
God for One's Own Purposes
By Creating "god" Into Our Own "Acceptable"
Image - Ongoing Idolatry*

1 Corinthians 10:14 "Therefore, my beloved, flee from idolatry"

2 Peter 2:1–3 "But false prophets also arose among the people, just as there will be false teachers among you, who will secretly bring in destructive heresies, even denying the Master"

1. Personal Motivator - Silence on Sin, Positive Thinking, Unity Over Holiness, Intolerant Tolerance, Evolving Morality (Not "Woe to you", Matthew 23)
2. Smooth-Talking, Attractional, Popular, & Loved Jesus (No Offense, Absolute Truth Statements - John 6:66; Not Despised & Rejected, Isaiah 55:3)
3. Good Teacher, Wise Man - Doubting or Ignoring Jesus' Divinity (Not, "I and the Father are one" John 10:30
4. Physical Healer - Wanting Miracles More than God Himself (Not spiritual "good news", "sight", and "liberty" Luke 4:20-30)
5. Giver of Abundant Life - Earthly Focused, Treasures of Earth (Not "Set your mind on things above" - Colossians 3:2)
6. Universal Salvation - All Go to Heaven, No Hell (Not "eternal punishment" and "eternal fire" Matthew 25:41, 46)
7. Self-Improvement - Change Oneself (Not Holy Spirit's Repentance and Sanctification, Galatians 3:3)
8. Self-Love and Satisfaction (Not, "Let him deny himself" Matthew 16:24)
9. Self-Rule - Obey Experiences, Emotions, and Opinions (Not "Obey God rather than men", Acts 5:29)
10. Servant of Mankind's Will, Genie-Like (Not God's "Will

Be Done", Matthew 6:10, 26:42)

WHAT DOES THE BIBLE SAY ABOUT CHRISTMAS?

What is Christmas? Christmas is a Christian day of celebration (December 25th) in honor of the birth of Jesus Christ. This event is significant to Christians as it is when God the Father sent His Son Jesus Christ in the flesh (incarnation), to reveal Himself and pay the price of our sin.

What is the true meaning of Christmas? Christmas for many people is a time of family gatherings, feasting, gift-giving, and traditional memory making. While these things themselves are good, the true meaning of Christmas is focused on the birth and appearance of Jesus Christ. We must be careful not to get distracted away from Jesus in the midst of the busyness of the Christmas season.

Why did Jesus say He was born? Jesus explains that "for this purpose I was born and for this purpose I have come into the world—to bear witness to the truth. Everyone who is of the truth listens to my voice" (John 18:37 ESV). Jesus was born to show us who He is, to teach us the truth about God, to provide a way of salvation through His sinless life, sacrificial death, and powerful resurrection.

What happened on Christmas day? The day of Jesus' birth was unusual in both its humility and majesty. Jesus was born in Bethlehem, the city of David, due to the Roman census/ registration, but ultimately as a fulfillment of prophecy (Micah 5:2, Matthew 2:1-6, Luke 2:1-5). Mary gave birth to Jesus in a stable, wrapped in cloth, and laid to rest in an animal feeding trough (Luke 1:6-8). Simultaneous with Jesus' humble birth was a magnificent and supernatural announcement by the angel of the Lord to shepherds (Luke 2:8-20) along with a multitude of angels proclaiming "Glory to God in the highest, and on earth peace among those with whom he is pleased!" (Luke 2:14 ESV)

What happened after Jesus' birth? After Jesus was born, he went through Jewish ceremonial traditions (Luke 2:21-38). His encounter with Simeon and Anna in the temple further evidenced that he was the way of "salvation" and "redemption." After Jesus' birth, wise men traveled from the east, following a star, to meet and worship Jesus. At this point Jesus was residing in a house, not at a stable, and the wise men made valuable offerings of gold, frankincense and myrrh, further attesting to Jesus' divine nature (Matthew 2:1-12). Because of the wise men's testimony of Jesus' fulfillment of prophecy, King Herod sought to murder Jesus by killing all of the young children in Bethlehem. Thankfully, God has warned Mary and Joseph to flee to Egypt with Jesus where they remained until the death of King Herod. Once the angel of the Lord told Joseph, they returned to Nazareth as another fulfillment of Scripture (Matthew 2:13-23, Luke 2:39-40)

Was Christmas really on December 25th? Although there are some very good historical reasons for the date of December 25th, ultimately we do not know the exact date of Jesus' birth. The most important details about Jesus' birth are given within the biblical accounts. Since the specific date is not shared, it is not a crucial issue of the Christian faith.

Where did all of the Christmas traditions come from? Christmas traditions and practices vary over time and culture. Some have significant connections in trying to create helpful celebrations that correlate with Christian truths, others simply arise from familial and cultural norms.

Should Christians celebrate Christmas? God warns Christians not to argue about particular days of celebration (Colossians 2:16-17), but that when making daily decisions in life we are reminded that in "whatever you do, do all to the glory of God" (1 Corinthians 10:31). We are also warned that "whatever does not proceed from faith is sin" (Romans 14:23). Although the Bible does not prescribe the regular, ceremonial remembrance of Jesus' birth (as it does with Jesus' death, burial and resurrection through the Lord's Supper, 1 Corinthians 11:17-34), Christians should daily celebrate Jesus in their drawing near to Him. In addition to our daily celebration of Christ, Christians have the freedom to celebrate Jesus' birth on Christmas as well if it builds up their faith (1 Corinthians 10:23).

"Therefore let no one pass judgment on you in questions of food and drink, or with regard to a festival or a new moon or a Sabbath. [17] These are a shadow of the things to come, but the substance belongs to Christ." (Colossians 2:16-17 ESV)

Why did Jesus have to be both God and human? Although this concept of Jesus being simultaneously human and deity (God) is difficult to grasp, it is a biblical and essential fact. Jesus' birth "under the law" allows the redemption, or purchase, of mankind from under the law. Only a perfect human (Jesus) would be capable and sufficient to keep and fulfill the law. Jesus' incarnation (coming in the flesh) allows a way for humans to be adopted as God's forever children.

Jesus' incarnation also allowed for his shedding of blood and death because "under the law almost everything is purified with blood, and without the shedding of blood there is no forgiveness of sins." (Hebrews 9:22) Unfortunately, the blood of animals is insufficient to atone for sin (Hebrews 10:4), so only the shed blood of a perfect God-man could provide a way of salvation.

Jesus' incarnation allowed him to sympathize with our

temptations and trials, yet Jesus remained perfect, holy, and without sin (Hebrews 4:15). Jesus came in the flesh to show and teach us the Truth: that Jesus and God the Father are one (John 10:30, 14:8-11) and that Jesus is the only way of salvation (John 14:6; Acts 4:12). World religions and cults teach that salvation can be found by good works, by being "good enough." The reality is that only Jesus, the God-man, is perfect and able to provide a way for salvation.

But when the fullness of time had come, God sent forth his Son, born of woman, born under the law, to redeem those who were under the law, so that we might receive adoption as sons. (Galatians 4:4-5)

For our sake he made him to be sin who knew no sin, so that in him we might become the righteousness of God. (2 Corinthians 5:21)

Jesus said to him, "I am the way, and the truth, and the life. No one comes to the Father except through me." (John 14:6)

And there is salvation in no one else, for there is no other name under heaven given among men by which we must be saved." (Acts 4:12 ESV)

Why is Christmas so important? Jesus is not simply the "reason for the season," He is the reason for life and for living. It is our hope and prayer that through this resource you discover or deepen in the love of Christ this Christmas!

What are the prophecies about Christmas? The prophecies about Jesus' birth and life are numerous, but here are a few:
1. **Offspring of a Woman** – Genesis 3:15, Luke 2:7, Revelation 12:5
2. **Offspring of Abraham** – Genesis 18:18, Acts 3:25, Matthew 1:1, Luke 3:34
3. **Offspring of Isaac** – Genesis 17:19, Matthew 1:2, Luke 3:34
4. **Offspring of Jacob** – Numbers 24:17, Genesis 28:14, Luke 3:34, Matthew 1:2

5. **Descended from the Tribe of Judah** – Genesis 49:10, Luke 3:33, Matthew 1:2-3
6. **Heir to the Throne of David** – Isaiah 9:7, 11:1-5, 2 Sam 7:13, Jer 23:5, Matt1:1,6, Luke 1:32-33
7. **Born in Bethlehem** – Micah 5:2, Matthew 2:1, Luke 2:4-7
8. **Time of Birth** – Daniel 9:25, Luke 2:1-2, 2:3-7
9. **Born of a Virgin** – Isaiah 7:14, Matthew 1:18, Luke 1:26-35
10. **Slaughter of Infants** – Jeremiah 31:15, Matthew 2:16-18
11. **Escape into Egypt** – Hosea 11:1, Matthew 2:14-15

How did Mary become pregnant with Jesus? The angel Gabriel (who has already announced the birth of John the Baptist to Zechariah and Elizabeth, Luke 1:5-24, 1:57-80) was sent by God to Nazareth to tell Mary that although she was a virgin, she would be pregnant with Jesus (Luke 1:26-56). Gabriel said "Do not be afraid, Mary, for you have found favor with God. [31] And behold, you will conceive in your womb and bear a son, and you shall call his name Jesus. [32] He will be great and will be called the Son of the Most High. And the Lord God will give to him the throne of his father David, [33] and he will reign over the house of Jacob forever, and of his kingdom there will be no end." (Luke 1:30-33 ESV)

Mary did not understand how this could be, but Gabriel assured her that "The Holy Spirit will come upon you, and the power of the Most High will overshadow you; therefore the child to be born will be called holy—the Son of God. [36] And behold, your relative Elizabeth in her old age has also conceived a son, and this is the sixth month with her who was called barren. [37] For nothing will be impossible with God." (Luke 1:35-37 ESV) Joseph was also told by an angel (Matthew 1:18-25) that "Joseph, son of David, do not fear to take Mary as your wife, for that which is conceived in her is from the Holy Spirit. She will bear a son, and you shall call his name Jesus, for he will save his people from their sins." (Matthew 1:21 ESV)

Mary's response to this amazing news? True Faith. "And Mary said, 'Behold, I am the servant of the Lord; let it be to me according to your word.'" (Luke 1:38) Upon sharing the news with her relative Elizabeth, Mary rejoiced and sang! (Luke 1:39-56) May we all sing and celebrate in a similar manner over the birth, life, death, and resurrection of Jesus!

What should I do about Christmas?
BELOW are some helpful answers...

Look to Jesus and Find Joy in Christ

And an angel of the Lord appeared to them, and the glory of the Lord shone around them, and they were filled with great fear. And the angel said to them, **"Fear not, for behold, I bring you good news of great joy that will be for all the people**. For unto you is born this day in the city of David a Savior, who is Christ the Lord. And this will be a sign for you: you will find a baby wrapped in swaddling cloths and lying in a manger." And suddenly there was with the angel a multitude of the heavenly host praising God and saying, "Glory to God in the highest, and on earth peace among those with whom he is pleased!" (Luke 2:9-14 ESV)

The Joy in Christ Test:

ASK YOURSELF - *Is your heart cold or hardened towards God?*
- Formal & routine worship. Going through the motions.
- Boredom or carelessness towards church and fellowship.
- No desire to talk about spiritual things.
- Bondage to sin: knowing a practice is sinful, but not caring enough to put an end to it.
- Out of control anger in thoughts, words, or actions.
- Selfish or critical attitude.
- Little interest or action in studying God's Word.
- Lack of desire for prayer. Seeing prayer as a duty.
- No interest or boredom in seeing people come to know Christ
- Sacrificially giving of your time, talents, or treasures. Feeling like you "have to" instead of "get to."

- Little desire to become more holy (sanctification). A decreasing conscience about sinfulness.
- Praying almost exclusively for yourself.
- Caring about the offense of others more than the offense of God.
- Faking it. Not being real, genuine, and open about your life.

Three Steps to JOY in Christ...

1. Repent and Draw Near to the Christ Child (James 4:8-10) Draw near to God, and he will draw near to you. Cleanse your hands, you sinners, and purify your hearts, you double-minded. [9] Be wretched and mourn and weep. Let your laughter be turned to mourning and your joy to gloom. [10] Humble yourselves before the Lord, and he will exalt you.

2. Believe in and know the Christ Child (Mark 9:22-24) "But if you can do anything, have compassion on us and help us." [23] And Jesus said to him, "'If you can'! All things are possible for one who believes." [24] Immediately the father of the child cried out and said, "I believe; help my unbelief!"

3. Delight in the Christ Child (Romans 7:21-25) So I find it to be a law that when I want to do right, evil lies close at hand. [22] **For I delight in the law of God, in my inner being**, [23] but I see in my members another law waging war against the law of my mind and making me captive to the law of sin that dwells in my members. [24] Wretched man that I am! Who will deliver me from this body of death? [25] Thanks be to God through Jesus Christ our Lord! So then, I myself serve the law of God with my mind, but with my flesh I serve the law of sin.

Rediscover the Gift of Christmas
(Isaiah 7:14 & Isaiah 9:6-7 ESV)

He Is Immanuel – God With Us

Isaiah 7:14 therefore the Lord himself will give you a sign. Behold, the virgin shall conceive and bear a son, and shall call his name

Immanuel.

Is God with you? Do you know it? Do you feel it? Are you sure?

    1. **No?** Fix it. Do Something. Stop Waiting. Seek Him.
(Deut. 4:29) you will seek the LORD your God and you will find him, if you search after him with all your heart and with all your soul.

- **Yes?** Live it. Be Encouraged. Draw Closer. You Are Not Alone. (James 4:8) Draw near to God, and he will draw near to you. Cleanse your hands, you sinners, and purify your hearts, you double-minded.

He Is Your Wonderful Counselor *Where do you go for advice? Answers? Solutions?*
(Isaiah 9:6) For to us a child is born, to us a son is given; and the government shall be upon his shoulder, and his name shall be called Wonderful Counselor

He Is Mighty God *Whose strength do you trust in? Seek Out? Act In? Daily?*
(2 Corinthians 12:10) For when I am weak, then I am strong.

He Is Everlasting Father *Where Is Your Focus? On Yourself? On Others? On World?*
Past, Present or Future? Temporary or eternal?
(Hebrews 13:8) Jesus Christ is the same yesterday & today & forever.

He Is Prince of Peace
What is your source of peace? Contentment? Stability? Hope?
(Isaiah 9:7) Of the increase of his government and of peace there will be no end, on the throne of David and over his kingdom, to establish it and to uphold it with justice and with righteousness from this time forth and forevermore. The zeal of the LORD of hosts will do this.

5 Gifts of Christ This Christmas:

Let His Names Live In Your Life!

- Draw Near Immanuel – Read, Hear, Obey His Bible
- Go to Christ with Your Problems – Speak in Prayer
- Rely on Mighty God – Be Weak & Dependent
- Look to Everlasting Father – Turn Your Attention
- Rest in the Prince of Peace – Hope in His Plan

Remember that Jesus Is
The Ultimate Gift
(Matthew 1 & 2, Luke 1 & 2 ESV)

7 Truths About Gifts

1. **Gifts are Purposed** "I am Gabriel. I stand in the presence of God, and I was sent to speak to you and to bring you this good news." Luke 1:19

2. **Gifts are Planned** The book of the genealogy of Jesus Christ, the son of David, the son of Abraham. Matthew 1:1, 17

3. **Gifts are Promised** All this took place to fulfill what the Lord had spoken by the prophet: 23 "Behold, the virgin shall conceive and bear a son, and they shall call his name Immanuel" (which means, God with us). Matt 1:22-23

4. **Gifts are Surprising** And Mary said to the angel, "How will this be, since I am a virgin?" 35 And the angel answered her, "The Holy Spirit will come upon you, and the power of the Most High will overshadow you; therefore the child to be born will be called holy-the Son of God." Luke 1:34-35

5. **Gifts are Expressive and Relational** "She will bear a son, and you shall call his name Jesus, for he will save his people

from their sins." Matthew 1:21

- "he will reign over the house of Jacob forever, and of his kingdom there will be no end." Luke 1:33

6. **Gifts are Loving** "Greetings, O favored one, the Lord is with you!" Luke 1:28

- "For nothing will be impossible with God." Luke 1:37

7. **Gifts are Free** "Glory to God in the highest, and on earth peace among those with whom he is pleased!" Luke 2:14

- And Mary said, "Behold, I am the servant of the Lord; let it be to me according to your word." And the angel departed from her." Luke 1:38

7 Practices With Gifts

1. **Anticipate the Gift** They told him, "In Bethlehem of Judea, for so it is written by the prophet: 6 "'And you, O Bethlehem, in the land of Judah, are by no means least among the rulers of Judah; for from you shall come a ruler who will shepherd my people Israel.'" (Matthew 2:5-6)

2. **Seek the Gift** Now after Jesus was born in Bethlehem of Judea in the days of Herod the king, behold, wise men from the east came to Jerusalem, 2 saying, "Where is he who has been born king of the Jews? For we saw his star when it rose and have come to worship him." (Matthew 2:1-2)

- After listening to the king, they went on their way. And behold, the star that they had seen when it rose went before them until it came to rest over the place where the child was. (Matthew 2:9)

3. **Rejoice in the Gift** When they saw the star, they rejoiced exceedingly with great joy. (Matt 2:10)

4. **Enjoy the Gift** And going into the house they saw the child with Mary his mother, and they fell down and worshiped him. (Matthew 2:11)

5. **Appreciate the Gift** Then, opening their treasures, they offered him gifts, gold and frankincense and myrrh. (Matthew 2:11)

6. **Use the Gift** And being warned in a dream not to return to Herod, they departed to their own country by another way. Matthew 2:12

7. **Share the Gift** But you will receive power when the Holy Spirit has come upon you, and you will be my witnesses in Jerusalem and in all Judea and Samaria, and to the end of the earth. (Acts 1:8)

WHAT DOES THE BIBLE SAY ABOUT EASTER?

What is Easter? Easter is a Christian holiday that is dedicated towards the celebration of Jesus' death, burial, and resurrection. In America and other places, this holiday has been transformed in recent history into a commercialized day that is focused on by many towards candy, gifts, egg-hunting games, the Easter bunny, and family gatherings.

What is the true meaning of Easter? The true meaning of Easter is a celebration of Jesus' sacrificial death on the cross and resurrection from the grave in order to provide a way of salvation through the forgiving of sin.

- Romans 10:9 "if you confess with your mouth that Jesus is Lord and believe in your heart that God raised him from the dead, you will be saved." (ESV)

Why did Jesus come to die? Jesus came to live out and show His truth and love. Jesus explains that "For this purpose I was born and for this purpose I have come into the world—to bear witness to the truth" (John 18:37). Jesus' death is a sacrifice in order to bring those who believe into a right relationship with God. "God shows his love for us in that while we were still sinners, Christ died for us" (Romans 5:8). There is no access to God in Heaven without Jesus' death and resurrection.

What happened on Easter? What happened after Jesus' resurrection? The Friday before Easter, Jesus was falsely accused, tortured, and executed by crucifixion (a slow method of killing by hanging, impaled with nails on wooden beams). After Jesus' death, He was buried, and three days later, on Easter, Jesus was resurrected to life. He then physically appeared to hundreds of people, showing His power and wisdom before ascending back into Heaven (John 18-21 & 1 Corinthians 15).

What is the Lenten season all about? Do Christians have to celebrate it? The Bible nowhere commands Christians to celebrate Lent. For those who choose to celebrate Lent, it is designed as a 40-day period of dedicated towards fasting and repentance leading into Easter. Its purpose is to prepare and remind Christians of the celebration of Jesus' death and resurrection.

Where did all of the Easter traditions come from? Should Christians celebrate Easter? Many of the Easter traditions originated in cultural traditions of the past. God warns Christians not to argue about particular days of celebration (Colossians 2:16-17), but that when making daily decisions in life, we are reminded that in "whatever you do, do all to the glory of God" (1 Corinthians 10:31). We are also warned that "whatever does not proceed from faith is sin" (Romans 14:23). The Bible does call Christians to a regular, ceremonial remembrance of Jesus' death, burial and resurrection through the Lord's Supper (1 Corinthians 11:17-34), but not necessarily through an Easter holiday. Christians should daily celebrate Jesus in their drawing near to Him. Christians have the freedom to celebrate Jesus' death, burial, and resurrection on Easter as well if it builds up their faith (1 Corinthians 10:23).

- "Therefore let no one pass judgment on you in questions of food and drink, or with regard to a festival or a new moon or a Sabbath. These are a shadow of the things to come, but the substance belongs to Christ." (Colossians 2:16-17)

Why did Jesus have to be both God and human? Although this concept of Jesus being simultaneously human and deity (God) is difficult to grasp, it is a biblical and essential fact. Jesus' birth "under the law" allows the redemption, or purchase, of mankind from under the law (God's perfect standard). Only a perfect human (Jesus) would be capable and sufficient to keep and fulfill the law. Jesus' incarnation (coming in the flesh) and sacrificial, substitutionary death allows a way for humans to be adopted as God's forever children through the paying of the penalty for sin.

Jesus' incarnation also allowed for his shedding of blood and death because "under the law almost everything is purified with blood, and without the shedding of blood there is no forgiveness of sins" (Hebrews 9:22). Unfortunately, the blood of animals is insufficient to sacrificially atone for sin (Hebrews 10:4), so only the shed blood of a perfect God-man could provide a way of salvation.

Jesus' incarnation allowed him to sympathize with our temptations and trials, yet Jesus remained perfect, holy, and without sin (Hebrews 4:15). Jesus came in the flesh to show and teach us the Truth: that Jesus and God the Father are one (John 10:30, 14:8-11) and that Jesus is the only way of salvation (John 14:6; Acts 4:12). World religions and cults teach that salvation can be found by good works or by being "good enough." The reality is that only Jesus, the God-man, is perfect and able to provide a way for salvation.

- But when the fullness of time had come, God sent forth his Son, born of woman, born under the law, to redeem those who were under the law, so that we might receive adoption as sons. (Galatians 4:4-5)
- For our sake he made him to be sin who knew no sin, so that in him we might become the righteousness of God. (2 Corinthians 5:21)
- Jesus said to him, "I am the way, and the truth, and the life. No one comes to the Father except through me. (John 14:6)
- And there is salvation in no one else, for there is no other name under heaven given among men by which we must be saved." (Acts 4:12 ESV)

Why is Easter so important? Jesus is not simply the "reason for the season," He is the reason for life and for living. It is our hope and prayer that you deepen in the love of Christ this Easter!

What are the prophecies about Easter? The prophecies about Jesus' death, burial, and resurrection are numerous, but here are a few:

1. **Triumphal Entry** – Zechariah 9:9, Isaiah 62:11, John 12:13-14, Matthew 21:1-11
2. **Betrayed by a Friend** – Psalm 41:9, Mark 14:10
3. **Sold for 30 Pieces of Silver, Potter's Field** – Zechariah 11:12-13, Matthew 26:15, 27:6-7
4. **Judas' Position Replaced** – Psalm 109:7, Acts 1:18-20
5. **False Witnesses' Accused Him** – Psalm 27:12, Matthew 26:60-61
6. **Silent When Accused** – Isaiah 53:5, Matthew 26:62-63
7. **Struck and Spit Upon** – Isaiah 50:6, Mark 14:65
8. **Hated Without Cause** – Psalm 69:4, John 15:23
9. **Suffered Vicariously** – Isaiah 53:4, Matthew 8:16-17
10. **Hands and Feet Pierced** – Psalm 22:16, John 20:27
11. **Crucified with Sinners** – Isaiah 53:12, Matthew 27:38
12. **Mocked and Insulted** – Psalm 22:6-8, Matthew 27:39-40
13. **Given Gall and Vinegar** – Psalm 69:21, John 19:29
14. **Hears Prophetic Words Used as Mockery** – Psalm 22:8, Matthew 27:43
15. **Prays for His Enemies** – Psalm 109:4, Luke 23:34
16. **Side Pierced** – Zechariah 12:10, John 19:34
17. **Soldiers Cast Lots for His Clothes** – Psalm 22:18, Matthew 15:24
18. **Not a Bone to Be Broken** – Psalm 34:20, John 19:33
19. **Buried with the Rich** – Isaiah 53:9, Matthew 27:57-60
20. **Resurrection** – Psalm 16:10, Matthew 28:9
21. **Ascension into Heaven** – Psalm 68:18, Luke 24:50

Check out this helpful resource: *The Case for Easter* by Lee Strobel

Easter Week - *What Happened, Day by Day*

If you have ever wondered what happened during each day of Easter week, I hope that you find this summary helpful. Be sure to look up and read the verses to see how amazing Jesus is!

Palm Sunday - On a Sunday, almost 2,000 years ago, as Jesus approached His crucifixion and resurrection, Jesus' presence "stirred up" the whole city of Jerusalem as He was worshiped with the words "Hosanna to the Son of David! Blessed is He who comes in the name of the Lord! Hosanna in the highest!" (Matthew 21:8-11). May we worship Jesus today!

Monday - On a Monday, almost 2,000 years ago, as Jesus approached His crucifixion and resurrection, "all the people were hanging on his words" (Luke 19:48). May we do the same today!

Tuesday - On a Tuesday, almost 2,000 years ago, as Jesus approached His crucifixion and resurrection, many nonbelievers sought to entrap and trick Jesus. Upon hearing Jesus' truth-filled answers and divine wisdom, His enemies "marveled" (Matthew 22:22) and the crowds were "astonished" (Matthew 22:33). May we marvel at and be astonished by our wondrous Jesus!

Wednesday - On a Wednesday, almost 2,000 years ago, as Jesus approached His crucifixion and resurrection, His enemies came against Him for His death, but crowds came to Him for His words of life! (Luke 21:37-22:2). May we come to Jesus for life today!

Thursday - On a Thursday, almost 2,000 years ago, as Jesus approached His crucifixion and resurrection, Judas betrayed Jesus and His other disciples disappointed Him. May we "watch and pray that" we likewise "do not enter into temptation" (Matthew 26:41).

Good Friday - On a Friday, almost 2,000 years ago, as Jesus was crucified, He proclaimed "Father, forgive them, for they know not what they do" (Luke 23:34). May we daily repent of our ignorant and willful sin against our Savior and hear His promise to true believers that "you will be with me in paradise" (Luke 23:43).

Saturday - On a Saturday, almost 2,000 years ago, as Jesus approached His resurrection, nonbelievers sought to deny Jesus' deity and to stop His fame (Matthew 27:62-66), but no-one and no-thing could prevent Jesus' resurrection. May we rejoice that nothing can "separate us from the love of Christ" (Romans 8:35).

Easter Sunday - On a Sunday, almost 2,000 years ago, after Jesus' crucifixion and resurrection, people who encountered the resurrected Jesus felt their "hearts burn within" them while Jesus talked with them and opened the Scriptures to them (Luke 24:32). May Jesus open our hearts, minds, and spirits to celebrate His presence with us through His Spirit and His Word! "The Lord has risen indeed!" (Luke 24:34) May we long for the day when He returns, but until that day, may we be worshipping Him "with great joy" and "continually...blessing God" (Luke 24:52).

JESUS' FINAL WORDS FROM THE CROSS

1st Word from the Cross - Luke 23:34 "Father forgive them, for they do not know what they do.

2nd Word from the Cross -Luke 23:43 "Today you will be with me in paradise"

3rd Word from the Cross - John 19:26-27 "Jesus saw His own mother, and the disciple standing near whom He loved. He said to His mother, Woman, behold your son.' Then He said to the disciple, 'Behold your mother.'"

4th Word from the Cross - Mark 15:34 "And at the ninth hour, Jesus shouted in a loud voice, 'Eloi, Elon, lama sabachthani?' which is translated, My God, my God, why have you forsaken me?"

5th Word from the Cross - John 19:28 "He said, 'I thirst.'"

6th Word from the Cross - Luke 23:46 "Speaking in a loud voice, Jesus said, Father, into your hands I commit my spirit."

7th Word from the Cross - John 19:30 "Jesus said, 'It is finished."

WHAT DOES THE BIBLE SAY ABOUT THE NAMES OF SATAN?

The Names of The Evil
One - Who Is He?

The Accuser. Your Adversary. Angel of the Abyss/Pit (Abaddon, Apollyon). The Antichrist. Beelzebul (The Prince/ Ruler of Demons, Lord of Flies, Lord of Dung). Belial. Day Star (In Latin, Lucifer, son of Dawn). The Deceiver. The Devil. The Dragon. The Enemy. The Evil One. The Father of Lies. King of Tyre (Anointed Guardian Cherub). A Murderer from the Beginning. Prince of Power of the Air. A Roaring Lion. The Ruler/god of this World/Age. Satan. The Serpent. Slanderer. The Tempter. The Thief. The Wolf.

The Antichrist
- 2 John 7 "For many deceivers have gone out into the world, those who do not confess the coming of Jesus Christ in the flesh. Such a one is the deceiver and the antichrist."
- 1 John 2:18 "Children, it is the last hour, and as you have heard that antichrist is coming, so now many antichrists have come. Therefore we know that it is the last hour."
- 1 John 2:22 "Who is the liar but he who denies that Jesus is the Christ? This is the antichrist, he who denies the Father and the Son."

Devil, The Accuser, Slanderer

- Matthew 4:1 "Then Jesus was led up by the Spirit into the wilderness to be tempted by the devil."
- Matthew 25:41 "Then he will say to those on his left, 'Depart from me, you cursed, into the eternal fire prepared for the devil and his angels.'"
- Revelation 12:10 "And I heard a loud voice in heaven, saying, 'Now the salvation and the power and the kingdom of our God and the authority of his Christ have come, for the accuser of our brothers has been thrown down, who accuses them day and night before our God.'"

The Dragon

- Revelation 12:3 "And another sign appeared in heaven: behold, a great red dragon, with seven heads and ten horns, and on his heads seven diadems."
- Revelation 20:2–3 "And he seized the dragon, that ancient serpent, who is the devil and Satan, and bound him for a thousand years, and threw him into the pit, and shut it and sealed it over him, so that he might not deceive the nations any longer, until the thousand years were ended. After that he must be released for a little while."

The Enemy, Your Adversary, A Roaring Lion
- Matthew 13:39 "and the enemy who sowed them is the devil. The harvest is the end of the age"
- 1 Peter 5:8 "Be sober-minded; be watchful. Your adversary the devil prowls around like a roaring lion, seeking someone to devour."

The Evil One
- John 17:15 "I do not ask that you take them out of the world, but that you keep them from the evil one."
- Matthew 13:19 "When anyone hears the word of the kingdom and does not understand it, the evil one comes and snatches away what has been sown in his heart. This is what was sown along the path."

The Father of Lies, Liar, The Deceiver
- John 8:44 "You are of your father the devil, and your will is to do your father's desires. He was a murderer from the beginning, and does not stand in the truth, because there is no truth in him. When he lies, he speaks out of his own character, for he is a liar and the father of lies."
- 2 John 7 "For many deceivers have gone out into the world, those who do not confess the coming of Jesus Christ in the flesh. Such a one is the deceiver and the antichrist."
- Revelation 12:9 "And the great dragon was thrown down, that ancient serpent, who is called the devil and Satan, the deceiver of the whole world—he was thrown down to the earth, and his angels were thrown down with him."

Murderer
- John 8:44 "You are of your father the devil, and your will is to do your father's desires. He was a murderer from the beginning, and does not stand in the truth, because there is no truth in him. When he lies, he speaks out of his own character, for he is a liar and the father of lies."
- 1 John 3:15 "Everyone who hates his brother is a murderer, and you know that no murderer has eternal life abiding in him."

The Prince/Ruler of Demons, Beelzebul, Lord of Flies, Lord of Dung

- Matthew 9:34 "But the Pharisees said, 'He casts out demons by the prince of demons.'"
- Matthew 10:25 "It is enough for the disciple to be like his teacher, and the servant like his master. If they have called the master of the house Beelzebul, how much more will they malign those of his household."
- Matthew 12:24 "But when the Pharisees heard it, they said, 'It is only by Beelzebul, the prince of demons, that this man casts out demons.'"

Prince of Power of the Air

- Ephesians 2:1–3 "And you were dead in the trespasses and sins in which you once walked, following the course of this world, following the prince of the power of the air, the spirit that is now at work in the sons of disobedience— among whom we all once lived in the passions of our flesh, carrying out the desires of the body and the mind, and were by nature children of wrath, like the rest of mankind."

The Ruler/god of this World/Age

- John 14:30 "I will no longer talk much with you, for the ruler of this world is coming. He has no claim on me"
- John 12:31 "Now is the judgment of this world; now will the ruler of this world be cast out."
- John 16:11 "concerning judgment, because the ruler of this world is judged."
- 2 Corinthians 4:4 "In their case the god of this world has blinded the minds of the unbelievers, to keep them from seeing the light of the gospel of the glory of Christ, who is the image of God."
- 1 John 5:19 "We know that we are from God, and the whole world lies in the power of the evil one."

Satan, The Accuser, The Adversary

- 1 Chronicles 21:1 "Then Satan stood against Israel and incited

David to number Israel."
- Job 1:7 "The LORD said to Satan, 'From where have you come?' Satan answered the LORD and said, 'From going to and fro on the earth, and from walking up and down on it.'"
- Luke 10:18 "And he said to them, 'I saw Satan fall like lightning from heaven.'"

The Serpent, The Great Dragon
- Genesis 3:1,4 "Now the serpent was more crafty than any of the wild animals the LORD God had made. He said to the woman, 'Did God really say ...'"
- 2 Corinthians 11:3 "But I am afraid that as the serpent deceived Eve by his cunning, your thoughts will be led astray from a sincere and pure devotion to Christ."
- Revelation 12:9 "And the great dragon was thrown down, that ancient serpent, who is called the devil and Satan, the deceiver of the whole world—he was thrown down to the earth, and his angels were thrown down with him."
- Revelation 20:2–3 "And he seized the dragon, that ancient serpent, who is the devil and Satan, and bound him for a thousand years, and threw him into the pit, and shut it and sealed it over him, so that he might not deceive the nations any longer, until the thousand years were ended. After that he must be released for a little while. (ESV)

The Tempter
- Matthew 4:3 "And the tempter came and said to him, 'If you are the Son of God, command these stones to become loaves of bread.'"
- 1 Thessalonians 3:5 "For this reason, when I could bear it no longer, I sent to learn about your faith, for fear that somehow the tempter had tempted you and our labor would be in vain."

The Thief
- John 10:10 "The thief comes only to steal and kill and destroy. I came that they may have life and have it abundantly."

The Wolf

- John 10:12 "He who is a hired hand and not a shepherd, who does not own the sheep, sees the wolf coming and leaves the sheep and flees, and the wolf snatches them and scatters them."

Less Common (and Sometimes Debated) Names of Satan

Angel of the Abyss/Pit, Abaddon, Apollyon

- Revelation 9:11 "They have as king over them the angel of the bottomless pit. His name in Hebrew is Abaddon, and in Greek he is called Apollyon."

Belial

- 2 Corinthians 6:15 "What accord has Christ with Belial? Or what portion does a believer share with an unbeliever?"

Day Star (In Latin, Lucifer), son of Dawn

- Isaiah 14:12 "How you are fallen from heaven, O Day Star, son of Dawn! How you are cut down to the ground, you who laid the nations low!"
- Revelation 12:4 "His tail swept down a third of the stars of heaven and cast them to the earth. And the dragon stood before the woman who was about to give birth, so that when she bore her child he might devour it."
- 2 Peter 2:4 "For if God did not spare angels when they sinned, but cast them into hell and committed them to chains of gloomy darkness to be kept until the judgment"
- Jude 6 "And the angels who did not stay within their own position of authority, but left their proper dwelling, he has kept in eternal chains under gloomy darkness until the judgment of the great day"

King of Tyre, Anointed Guardian Cherub

- Ezekiel 28:12–13 "Son of man, raise a lamentation over the king of Tyre, and say to him, Thus says the Lord GOD: "You were the signet of perfection, full of wisdom and perfect in beauty. You were in Eden, the garden of God; every precious stone was your covering, sardius, topaz, and diamond, beryl, onyx, and jasper, sapphire, emerald, and carbuncle; and crafted in gold were your settings and your engravings. On the day that you were created they were prepared."

- Ezekiel 28:14–15 "You were an anointed guardian cherub. I placed you; you were on the holy mountain of God; in the midst of the stones of fire you walked. You were blameless in your ways from the day you were created, till unrighteousness was found in you."

WHAT DOES THE BIBLE SAY ABOUT THE WORKS OF SATAN?

Satan's Works - What Does He Do?
The Devil's Tactics & Schemes

2 Corinthians 2:11 "so that we would not be outwitted by Satan; for we are not ignorant of his designs." (ESV)

Arrogantly Resists God and Vainly Relies on Self

Ezekiel 28:17 "Your heart was proud because of your beauty; you corrupted your wisdom for the sake of your splendor. I cast you to the ground; I exposed you before kings, to feast their eyes on you."

- Isaiah 14:13 You said in your heart, 'I will ascend to heaven; above the stars of God I will set my throne on high; I will sit on the mount of assembly in the far reaches of the north"

Appeals to Fleshly Desires, Ambition, Covetousness, and Pride

Genesis 3 & 1 John 2:16–17 For all that is in the world—the desires of the flesh and the desires of the eyes and pride of life—is not from the Father but is from the world. And the world is passing away along with its desires, but whoever does the will of God abides forever."

Incites Pride in Numbers

1 Chronicles 21:1 "Then Satan stood against Israel and incited David to number Israel."

Travels Continuously Across the Earth
Job 1:7 "The LORD said to Satan, 'From where have you come?' Satan answered the LORD and said, 'From going to and fro on the earth, and from walking up and down on it.'"

Steals Away Earthly Possessions, Positions, and People
Job 1:10–11 "Have you not put a hedge around him and his house and all that he has, on every side? You have blessed the work of his hands, and his possessions have increased in the land. But stretch out your hand and touch all that he has, and he will curse you to your face."

Attacks Physical, Emotional, and Mental Health
Job 2:4–5 "Then Satan answered the LORD and said, 'Skin for skin! All that a man has he will give for his life. But stretch out your hand and touch his bone and his flesh, and he will curse you to your face.'"

Enters God's Presence to Attack Godly Followers
Zechariah 3:1 "Then he showed me Joshua the high priest standing before the angel of the LORD, and Satan standing at his right hand to accuse him."

Actively Tempts Us Away from Following God
Matthew 4:1-11 - Satan's Temptation of Jesus
· 2 Corinthians 2:11 "so that we would not be outwitted by Satan; for we are not ignorant of his designs"

Places False Believers Among True Believers
Matthew 13:24-30,36-43 "the enemy came and sowed weeds among the wheat...the weeds are the sons of the evil one and the enemy who sowed them is the devil"

Distracts Believers' Minds Towards Earthly Things

Matthew 16:22–23 "And Peter took him aside and began to rebuke him, saying, "Far be it from you, Lord! This shall never happen to you." But he turned and said to Peter, 'Get behind me, Satan! You are a hindrance to me. For you are not setting your mind on the things of God, but on the things of man.'"

Persistently Tempts by Twisting Scripture
Mark 1:13 "And he was in the wilderness forty days, being tempted by Satan. And he was with the wild animals, and the angels were ministering to him."

Prevents the Gospel from Being Understood and Believed
Mark 4:14–15 "The sower sows the word. And these are the ones along the path, where the word is sown: when they hear, Satan immediately comes and takes away the word that is sown in them."

Offers Shortcuts Away from God's Provision
Luke 4:3 "The devil said to him, 'If you are the Son of God, command this stone to become bread.'"

Baits You Towards Seeking Possessions, Power, and Prestige
Luke 4:6–7 "To you I will give all this authority and their glory, for it has been delivered to me, and I give it to whom I will. If you, then, will worship me, it will all be yours."

Tries to Get You to Manipulate God
Luke 4:9–10 "And he took him to Jerusalem and set him on the pinnacle of the temple and said to him, "If you are the Son of God, throw yourself down from here, for it is written, 'He will command his angels concerning you, to guard you,'"

Patiently Looks for Future Temptation Opportunities
Luke 4:13 "And when the devil had ended every temptation, he departed from him until an opportune time."

Prevents the Bible from Being Heard, Understood, Loved, and Believed.

Luke 8:12 "The ones along the path are those who have heard; then the devil comes and takes away the word from their hearts, so that they may not believe and be saved."

Enters Into (Possesses) Humans for His Purposes

Luke 22:3–6 "Then Satan entered into Judas called Iscariot, who was of the number of the twelve. He went away and conferred with the chief priests and officers how he might betray him to them. And they were glad, and agreed to give him money. So he consented and sought an opportunity to betray him to them in the absence of a crowd."

Spreads Hatred and Lies

John 8:44 "You are of your father the devil, and your will is to do your father's desires. He was a murderer from the beginning, and does not stand in the truth, because there is no truth in him. When he lies, he speaks out of his own character, for he is a liar and the father of lies."

Kills and Destroys

John 10:10 "The thief comes only to steal and kill and destroy. I came that they may have life and have it abundantly."

· Revelation 12:12 "Therefore, rejoice, O heavens and you who dwell in them! But woe to you, O earth and sea, for the devil has come down to you in great wrath, because he knows that his time is short!"

Provokes Betrayal Against God

John 13:2 "During supper, when the devil had already put it into the heart of Judas Iscariot, Simon's son, to betray him"

Dangerously Attacks the Followers of Jesus

John 17:15 "I do not ask that you take them out of the world, but that you keep them from the evil one."

Provides Pathways for Greed

Acts 5:3–4 "But Peter said, 'Ananias, why has Satan filled your heart to lie to the Holy Spirit and to keep back for yourself part of the proceeds of the land? While it remained unsold, did it not remain your own? And after it was sold, was it not at your disposal? Why is it that you have contrived this deed in your heart? You have not lied to man but to God.'"

Oppresses the Lost

Acts 10:38 "how God anointed Jesus of Nazareth with the Holy Spirit and with power. He went about doing good and healing all who were oppressed by the devil, for God was with him."

Works Against God's Work

Acts 13:10 "You son of the devil, you enemy of all righteousness, full of all deceit and villainy, will you not stop making crooked the straight paths of the Lord?"

Spiritually Blinds Unbelievers

Acts 26:18 " to open their eyes, so that they may turn from darkness to light and from the power of Satan to God, that they may receive forgiveness of sins and a place among those who are sanctified by faith in me.'"

• 2 Corinthians 4:4 "In their case the god of this world has blinded the minds of the unbelievers, to keep them from seeing the light of the gospel of the glory of Christ, who is the image of God."

Brings Physical Suffering to those Outside of Church

1 Corinthians 5:5 "you are to deliver this man to Satan for the destruction of the flesh, so that his spirit may be saved in the day of the Lord."

Entraps in Lust & Sexual Sin

1 Corinthians 7:5 "Do not deprive one another, except perhaps by agreement for a limited time, that you may devote yourselves to prayer; but then come together again, so that Satan may not tempt you because of your lack of self-control."

Enslaves with Bitterness and Unforgiveness

2 Corinthians 2:10–11 "Anyone whom you forgive, I also forgive. Indeed, what I have forgiven, if I have forgiven anything, has been for your sake in the presence of Christ, so that we would not be outwitted by Satan; for we are not ignorant of his designs."

Leads People to an Insincere & Impure Faith

2 Corinthians 11:3 "But I am afraid that as the serpent deceived Eve by his cunning, your thoughts will be led astray from a sincere and pure devotion to Christ."

Attracts Us to His False Appearance
2 Corinthians 11:14 "And no wonder, for even Satan disguises himself as an angel of light."

Tricks People to Believing He is All-Powerful, All-Knowing, and Good
2 Corinthians 11:13–15 "For such men are false apostles, deceitful workmen, disguising themselves as apostles of Christ. And no wonder, for even Satan disguises himself as an angel of light. So it is no surprise if his servants, also, disguise themselves as servants of righteousness. Their end will correspond to their deeds."

Harasses Believers
2 Corinthians 12:7 "So to keep me from becoming conceited because of the surpassing greatness of the revelations, a thorn was given me in the flesh, a messenger of Satan to harass me, to keep me from becoming conceited."

Encourages Anger, Laziness and Stinginess
Ephesians 4:26–28 "Be angry and do not sin; do not let the sun go down on your anger, and give no opportunity to the devil. Let the thief no longer steal, but rather let him labor, doing honest work with his own hands, so that he may have something to share with anyone in need."

Intentionally Plans for His Next Attack
Ephesians 6:11 "Put on the whole armor of God, that you may be able to stand against the schemes of the devil."

Wrestles Against Believers Indirectly through Others
Ephesians 6:12 "For we do not wrestle against flesh and blood, but against the rulers, against the authorities, against the cosmic powers over this present darkness, against the spiritual forces of

evil in the heavenly places."

Leads People Into Gluttony, Worldliness, & Shamefulness

Philippians 3:18–19 "For many, of whom I have often told you and now tell you even with tears, walk as enemies of the cross of Christ. Their end is destruction, their god is their belly, and they glory in their shame, with minds set on earthly things."

Stops Mission Work

1 Thessalonians 2:17–18 "But since we were torn away from you, brothers, for a short time, in person not in heart, we endeavored the more eagerly and with great desire to see you face to face, because we wanted to come to you—I, Paul, again and again—but Satan hindered us."

Empowers False Miracles

2 Thessalonians 2:9–10 "The coming of the lawless one is by the activity of Satan with all power and false signs and wonders, and with all wicked deception for those who are perishing, because they refused to love the truth and so be saved."

Condemns through Pride and Arrogance

1 Timothy 3:6 "He must not be a recent convert, or he may become puffed up with conceit and fall into the condemnation of the devil."

Seeks to Dishonor the Name and Reputation of Believers

1 Timothy 3:7 "Moreover, he must be well thought of by outsiders, so that he may not fall into disgrace, into a snare of the devil."

Encourages Laziness, Gossip, and Nosiness

1 Timothy 5:13–15 "Besides that, they learn to be idlers, going about from house to house, and not only idlers, but also gossips and busybodies, saying what they should not. So I would have younger widows marry, bear children, manage their households, and give the adversary no occasion for slander. For some have already strayed after Satan."

Manipulates and Controls Unbelievers for His Purpose

2 Timothy 2:26 "and they may come to their senses and escape from the snare of the devil, after being captured by him to do his will."

Enslaves Humanity Under a Fear of Death

Hebrews 2:14–15 "Since therefore the children share in flesh and blood, he himself likewise partook of the same things, that through death he might destroy the one who has the power of death, that is, the devil, and deliver all those who through fear of death were subject to lifelong slavery."

Flees from Faithful Resistance

James 4:7 "Submit yourselves therefore to God. Resist the devil, and he will flee from you."

Brings Suffering Against Saints

1 Peter 5:8–9 "Be sober-minded; be watchful. Your adversary

the devil prowls around like a roaring lion, seeking someone to devour. Resist him, firm in your faith, knowing that the same kinds of suffering are being experienced by your brotherhood throughout the world."

Appeals to Our Eyes, Flesh, and Pride

1 John 2:16 "For all that is in the world—the desires of the flesh and the desires of the eyes and pride of life—is not from the Father but is from the world."

Desires Us to Sin By Acting (Commission or Omission) On the Temptation

1 John 3:8 "Whoever makes a practice of sinning is of the devil, for the devil has been sinning from the beginning. The reason the Son of God appeared was to destroy the works of the devil."

Wants His Followers to Imitate His Example of Disobedience

1 John 3:10 "By this it is evident who are the children of God, and who are the children of the devil: whoever does not practice righteousness is not of God, nor is the one who does not love his brother."

Imprisons and Kills Faithful Saints

Revelation 2:10 "Do not fear what you are about to suffer. Behold, the devil is about to throw some of you into prison, that you may be tested, and for ten days you will have tribulation. Be faithful unto death, and I will give you the crown of life."

Births, Grows, and Encourages All False Religions & Cults

Revelation 2:12–13 "And to the angel of the church in Pergamum write: 'The words of him who has the sharp two-edged sword. 'I know where you dwell, where Satan's throne is. Yet you hold fast my name, and you did not deny my faith even in the days of Antipas my faithful witness, who was killed among you, where Satan dwells.'"

- 1 Corinthians 10:20 "No, I imply that what pagans sacrifice they offer to demons and not to God. I do not want you to be participants with demons."

Deceives the Whole World
Revelation 12:9 "And the great dragon was thrown down, that ancient serpent, who is called the devil and Satan, the deceiver of the whole world—he was thrown down to the earth, and his angels were thrown down with him."

Suffers Forever
Revelation 20:10 "and the devil who had deceived them was thrown into the lake of fire and sulfur where the beast and the false prophet were, and they will be tormented day and night forever and ever."

WHAT DOES THE BIBLE SAY ABOUT THE CHARACTER OF SATAN?

*WHAT DOES THE BIBLE
SAY SATAN IS LIKE?*

The Character & Attributes Of Satan

2 Corinthians 11:14 "even Satan disguises
himself as an angel of light." (ESV)

Why does Satan do what he does?
What are Satan's abilities?
What are Satan's motives?
What are Satan's goals?

Satan desires to elevate his image above God's image, by blinding and blurring our view of the image of God. The Evil One opposes your enjoyment, worship, and growth into God's image. The Devil's goal is to blend your image into his image, deceiving you into imitating his character rather than God's character.

1. **Singular Being (vs. God's Trinitarian Unity)**
2. **Limited Beauty (vs. God's Absolute Beauty)**

3. Cursed (vs. God as Blessed)
4. Created (vs. God as Creator & Preexistent)
5. Source of Death (vs. God as Source of Life)
6. Fallen (vs. God's Divinity)
7. Everlasting Destruction (vs. God from Everlasting)
8. Faithless (vs. God as Faithful)
9. Enslaving (vs. God's Freedom)
10. Evil (vs. God's Goodness)
11. Condemning (vs. God as Gracious & Merciful)
12. Unholy (vs. God's Holiness)
13. Dependent (vs. God's Independence)
14. Guilty (vs. God's Innocence)
15. Competitive (vs. God's Right Jealousy)
16. Judged (vs. God's as Judge
17. Hidden (vs. God as Knowable)
18. Hate (vs. God is Love)
19. Limited Power (vs. God's Omnipotence)
20. Limited Presence (vs. God's Omnipresence)
21. Limited Knowledge (vs. God's Omniscience)
22. Sinful (vs. God is Perfect)
23. Wicked (vs. God is Righteous)
24. Rebellious (vs. God is Sovereign)
25. Weak (vs. God's Strength)
26. Deceitful (vs. God as Truthful)
27. Manipulative (vs. God is Unchangeable)
28. Foolish (vs. God is Wise)
29. Worthless (vs. God is Worthy)
30. Under Wrath (vs. God's Wrath Upon Sin)

ABOUT THE AUTHOR

Dr. Jonathan Carl

Jonathan Carl grew up in the great state of Texas as the oldest of six kids. He graduated from the United States Military Academy at West Point and served in the U.S. Army as a tanker with a combat tour in Iraq in the early 2000s. He had the joy of journeying to Kentucky where he met and married his wonderful wife, Brittney. Several years later he became the lead pastor at South Fork Baptist Church where he has served for over a decade. He enjoyed the opportunities to study and earn his Master of Divinity and Doctor of Philosophy degrees in Evangelism & Missions from the Southern Baptist Theological Seminary. Jonathan & Brittney have four daughters (Sophia, Lydia, Alia & Mia) with whom they enjoy spending every spare minute they can.

HONEST BOOK REVIEWS NEEDED

I would love your feedback on this book and your Bible reading journey and resulting small group discussions. Your **genuine Amazon review** can be a great help to others who are seeking to encounter God through Bible reading and listening plans.

In addition to Amazon reviews, **social media sharing** is also a great way to encourage and resource others. As the Lord teaches and grows you in this journey, please consider telling others about any help this book was to you.

As always, this book and 10+ more are available for **free download (PDF)** and sharing on any of my below websites. I'm praying for Jesus' work in and through you!

In Christ, Jonathan Carl

God's answers about the battle of the followers of Christ against the unseen spiritual forces of evil. www.SpiritualWarfare.blog

Get answers to some of life's toughest questions! www.TrustworthyWord.com

Getting the Bible into people and people into the Bible via video! www.Bible.video

A place for Catholics to find biblical answers to their most common questions about the Catechism of the Catholic Church! www.Catholic.blog - helping people to answer the question: "Does the Catholic Catechism agree with or contradict the Bible?"

Free book downloads at the above links & kindle/print versions on Amazon @ www.amazon.com/author/jonathancarl

Sermons & teaching videos: www.youtube.com/@SouthFork and www.youtube.com/@trustworthyword

Printed in Dunstable, United Kingdom

67529958R10057